wake up curious

Wacuri Publishing

Wake Up Curious

Dan Spinner is an Executive and Life coach for clients from many countries across two continents. Dan has been a senior executive with a range of NGOs, including Hospitals and Universities and has helped raise over $300 million for charities and businesses. He uses an intuitive decision-making process that includes the Wacuri Method, which helps his clients achieve major breakthroughs in implementing their dreams. Along with his more traditional NGO work, Dan has been the CEO of the Deepak Chopra Foundation and a Senior Advisor to the Esalen Institute. Dan has a black belt in Aikido and has been studying and teaching this "way of harmony" for over 40 years, bringing its principles of flow and energy to his work and his clients.

wake up curious

The Wacuri Method of Five Minutes
a Day Meditation for Individual
and Collective Health, Wealth
and Happiness

Waterside Productions

Printed in the United States of America

First Printing, 2020

ISBN-13: 978-1-949003-23-9 print edition
ISBN-13: 978-1-949003-24-6 ebook edition
ISBN-13: 978-1-949003-25-3 audiobook edition

Waterside Productions
2055 Oxford Ave
Cardiff, CA 92007
www.waterside.com

Wacuri Publishing
3470 Shangri La Road
Lafayette, CA 94549
https://curious.live

Brad Burkhart, Publisher
Julie Perkins, Senior Research Advisor

THE LIBRARY OF CONGRESS HAS CATALOGED THE
PAPERBACK EDITION AS FOLLOWS:

Wake Up Curious / Dan Spinner.

CONTENTS

Foreword xi

Introduction 1

Chapter One: Why Wake Up Curious? 15

Power Flows Into the Moment 16

The Root of All Neurosis 18

Endlessly Creative Consciousness 19

A Breakthrough Method 20

Chapter Two: Flow Is A Deeper Connection 25

Encounters With the Natural World 27

The Truth Behind the Word 28

The Way of Harmony 31

Higher Order Information-Sharing 34

In the Flow 36

Harmony Is Our Natural State 40

Learn To Play With Life Force Energy 44

Get Cozy With Not Knowing 47

Chapter Three: Seeing Things Into Existence 51

The Natural Inclination of Mind 52

A Free-thinking Household 54

Visualizing Results 57

Flow, Intuition, and Synchronicity 62

A Higher Platform For Living 64

Chapter Four: Meditation For Busy People............69

   The Henry Hypothesis: "I Have Five Minutes" ..70

   Basic Structure and The Next Evolution...............74

   Lucid Dreaming, Lucid Awakening......................76

   Mindfulness In Its Many Forms...........................79

   Relation of Wacuri to Other Meditation
   Methods..83

   Verbalization and the Method 86

   The Case for Social Meditation 87

   Deeper Connections, Stronger Human Bonds.....89

**Chapter Five: Evolution's Secret: The Hunger
for What's New and Better** 95

   Enter Through the Imaginal Realm......................96

   The Primal Urge to Explore..................................98

   Social Curiosity, Social Media, and Social
   Intelligence...101

   A Benevolent Platform to Call Out Our
   Higher Nature 103

   The 5-Type Model of Curiosity 104

   A Trait Not Just A State 112

   Your Curiosity Has Been Hijacked.....................116

Chapter Six: Gateway to the Infinite......................121

   The Biofield: A New, Yet Ancient Concept........122

   Of Dogs, Cats and Trees.....................................124

   Take A Moment…..126

   The Boundary of Self and Other 128

   Individuality and Oneness 130

   Crazy Insanity… or Sheer brilliance?.................131

   How's that for a Zen koan? 134

Our "faulty" reality-making processes...............135
Alternative Realities: Embracing the
Non-Ordinary...138
The Extraordinary World That's Right
Beneath Your Nose 141

Chapter Seven: From Flatland to Wonderland.....147
The known and the unknown..............................148
Manifesting From A State of Flow 155
Flow Transforms Crisis Into Opportunity 157
The Democratization of Spirituality....................165
Creative Teams and Flow States...........................167
Leadership to the Nth Degree...............................173
Creative Problem-Solving in Flow 177
Curiosity In Organizations....................................180
The Wake Up Curious Community 186

**Chapter Eight: From Solo Meditation to
Cyber-Sangha** 189
A Persistent Delusion...190
The Better Part of Ourselves 194
Not Exactly Mindfulness or Meditation.............195
What's Unique About the Wacuri Method 199

**Chapter Nine: The Wacuri Method and
Technology**..205
The Wakuri Method 206
The Wacuri Journey: An overview.......................211
The Journey Guide..212
Breathing and Posture...214
Invitation and Invocation 215

Introduction to Subject 216
The Journey Proper 216
The Apotheosis, or "Moment of Awe" 219
Space of Appreciation 221
The Return to Everyday Living 222
Time to Share 223
The Afterglow of a Journey 225
A Sample Journey: The Consciousness of Cells .. 227

Chapter Ten: Wake Up Connected 235
The Impact of the Method 235
Light in the Face of Mortality, Wisdom in
the Face of Death 237
Imaginal Calisthenics 239
Sample Sharings 242
A Multiverse of Journeys 246

Chapter Eleven: Hallmarks of Awakening 249
Gaining An Internal Compass 251
Tapping Into A Greater Force 252
Self Knowledge and Surrender 255
Self-responsibility: Your Greatest Asset 256
Connected Co-Creative Intelligence 259
Stardust and Light 262

**Appendix A: Curious.live Platform Research
and Development** 267

Appendix B: The Journey Guide School 271

Thank You ! 279

FOREWORD

We are social creatures. Our reality exists in our relationship to one another. Yet many of us suffer from existential loneliness. As a result we end up feeling disconnected from the world and our fellow human beings, stuck in a vicious biofeedback loop of trauma and disorientation. This loop is both personal and collective, which makes it evermore difficult to escape. Surely we can and must do better. We need deeper connections with our self, with others, and with the universe. That is why we have created social meditation online.

~ Dan Spinner

INTRODUCTION

Some forms of meditation are all about the method. Others are all about the lineage. Still others revolve around a particular teacher whose charisma holds the community together. But at their core, all forms of meditation are meant to connect us with the deepest aspects of ourselves—so that we can expand our human experience by being more fully present and living with a greater sense of peace and connectivity.

The Wacuri Method of "social mediation for busy people" is a new kind of mediation—one that explicitly makes the meditation journey a shared experience. Wacuri's placement of meditation into a social context takes participants on a transmissive journey to explore the inner world, while providing the opportunity to share that experience in the presence of others immediately afterwards. Wacuri creates a digital sangha—a community of meditators, beginning through advanced in practice, who can support each other on our collective journey to be self-realized as human beings.

Belonging is a fundamental human need. We are now well aware of the data supporting the notion that loneliness kills,[1] while connection heals.[2] While each birth begins from a mother's womb, growing up we are taught that "we are born alone, and we die alone." We experience ourselves as separate, and the idea of separateness often increases as we go through institutionalized learning.

But what if the experience of separation is an illusion? And what happens when we shatter this illusion to realize that we are co-creating our individual and collective destinies? Is there data to support such contentions?

The main topics of this book, which are more fully explored in the chapters that follow, include the biofield, flow state, energetic transmission, non-local consciousness, neuroscience, existential loneliness, belonging, curiosity, and The Wacuri Method of social meditation. If any or all of these subject-matter are of interest to you, then you are precisely in the right place and at the right time.

Social meditation is essentially the shared experience of accessing Source and Higher Self. To that end, all

---

[1] Holt-Lunstad J, Smith TB, Baker M, Harris T, Stephenson D. (2015, Mar). Retrieved from https://www.ncbi.nlm.nih.gov/pubmed/25910392

[2] Am Psychol. (2017, Sep). Retrieved from https://www.ncbi.nlm .nih.gov/pubmed/28880099

Wacuri Journeys are designed to invoke a moment of awe or wonder about the guide's chosen topic. That moment occurs in the mind of participants who typically close their eyes during a journey, which helps enable transcending the "first attention," linked to language, thinking and the automatic assignment of labels and meanings. Journeyers engage the inner action of seeing, of witnessing in an imaginal realm which produces and simulates novel objects, peoples and ideas without any assignment of meaning or labels.

As the aperture of perception opens, like when we dream, our view of reality expands exponentially. Whatever you can imagine, you can see. You can be an eagle, or the entire universe. The boundaries are theoretically limitless. Being present in this state can be quite exhilarating. That, in turn, creates a sense of awe and wonder which evokes a special kind of bond between those who share the experience. In his 1757 treatise, "A Philosophical Enquiry into the Origin of Our Ideas of the Sublime and Beautiful," Irish philosopher Edmund Burke detailed how we feel the sublime (awe) not just during religious ritual or in communion with God, but in everyday perceptual experiences: hearing thunder, being moved by music, seeing repetitive patterns of light and dark. Awe was to be found in daily life.

In recent years, the scientific community has become interested in the physiology of awe and curiosity, as well as exploring how the shared experiences of energy and information tie us together. While meditation has generally been scientifically studied as an isolatory practice, researchers are now beginning to explore how shared meditative experiences may provide synchrony between people—for example, by examining brainwave synchrony. These types of "hyperscanning" studies[3] can be considered part of a growing discipline called biofield science—the study of fields of energy and information that guide the homeodynamic regulation of living systems.[4]

Biofield science extends us beyond the study of "life as chemistry" and helps us to more deeply understand the meaning and significance as "life as vibration," from cells to communities. Biofield scientists may choose to study the bioelectromagnetic emanations of cells and discover that manipulating voltage gradients across cell

---

[3] Neurosci Res. (2015, Jan). Retrieved from
https://www.ncbi.nlm.nih.gov/pubmed/25499683

[4] Kreitzer et al, Jain et al, Rubik et al, Daubenmier et al, Kafatos et al, Hammerschlag et al, Muehsam et al, Gronowicz et al, Mills et al, Radin et al, Warber et al, Hufford et al, Guarneri et al. (2015). Retrieved from
https://www.chi.is/biofield-science-and-healing-special-issue

membranes can grow new neural tissue.[5] Scientists may choose to study how biofield devices, such as pulsed electromagnetic field stimulation, generate healing from pain and bone repair.[6]

Biofield scientists also may choose to study the more subtle aspects of the biofield and relate them to healing. For example, researchers have conducted randomized controlled trials examining time-honored practices such as laying-on-of-hands and more modern "energy healing" practices such as Healing Touch—and how they impact cancer patients in terms of fatigue, depression, immune and hormone function.[7,8] Scientists are now reporting how adept energy healers can affect the size and migration of cancer tumors.[9,10]

---

[5] Curr Opin Genet Dev. Whited JL, Levin M. (2019, Aug). Retrieved from https://www.ncbi.nlm.nih.gov/pubmed/31442749

[6] Ann Biomed Eng. Daish C, Blanchard R, Fox K, Pivonka P, Pirogova E. (2018, Apr). Retrieved from https://www.ncbi.nlm.nih.gov/pubmed/29356996

[7] Jain S, Pavlik D, Distefan J, Bruyere RL, Acer J, Garcia R, Coulter I, Ives J, Roesch SC, Jonas W, Mills PJ. (2012, Feb). Retrieved from https://www.ncbi.nlm.nih.gov/pubmed/21823103

[8] Brain Behav Immun. Lutgendorf SK, Mullen-Houser E, Russell D, Degeest K, Jacobson G, Hart L, Bender D, Anderson B, Buekers TE, Goodheart MJ, Antoni MH, Sood AK, Lubaroff DM. (2010, Nov). Retrieved from https://www.ncbi.nlm.nih.gov/pubmed/?term=lutgendorf+preservation

[9] Evid Based Complement Alternat Med. Gronowicz G, Secor ER Jr, Flynn JR, Jellison ER, Kuhn LT. (2015). Retrieved from https://www.ncbi.nlm.nih.gov/pubmed/26113869

[10] Integr Cancer Ther. Yang P, Jiang Y, Rhea PR, Coway T, Chen D, Gagea M, Harribance SL, Cohen L. (2019 Jan-Dec). Retrieved from https://www.ncbi.nlm.nih.gov/pubmed/30947564

In all these cases, further study of the biofield plays an important role in understanding how the nature and quality of our vibrations — some measurable, and some yet too subtle to measure directly — affect our life and our health. We are beginning to expand our view of how living systems work, factoring growing evidence of an organizing energy field, composed of both measurable electromagnetic energy and subtle energy.

In the biofield view, human beings are an integral part of their environment rather than creatures that merely adapt to it. Consciousness is intimately related to notions of biofields or subtle energies that regulate health. In this view, health and wellbeing correspond to harmonious energy flow. Disease corresponds to disruption or chronic imbalances in this harmony, and healing is the restoration of harmony. Specific practices, including but not limited to meditation and yoga, are recommended to facilitate healing through influencing the practitioner's state of consciousness and subtle body. Experiences of energetic shifts and guided energetic practice can often foster a flow state — where a person is fully immersed in a feeling of energized focus and enjoyment in the process of an activity. This state is characterized by the complete absorption in what one does, and a resulting loss in one's sense of space and time. This type of state is also facilitated by experiences of energetic transmission — characterized by an experience of supra-conceptual and supra-physical information sharing. For eons, the yogis and sages of India have known the secrets of energetic transmission, which initiates profound self-healing and transformative processes from within.

A powerful transmission can be a life-shaping experience. Energetic transformation can happen directly and intentionally through shaktipat experiences with a spiritual teacher. But transmission can also happen in the context of group spiritual practice. Transmission, and the continued nurtance of the biofield of a practitioner, is perhaps the reason why meditation leaders such as the venerable Thich Nhat Hanh note the importance of spiritual community (sangha) in meditation practice:

"The presence of a sangha is a wonderful opportunity to allow the collective energy of the sangha to penetrate into our body and consciousness. We profit a lot from that collective energy. We can entrust ourselves to the sangha because the sangha is practicing, and the collective energy of mindfulness is strong. Although we can rely on the energy of mindfulness that is generated by our personal practice, sometimes it is not enough.

But if you know how to use that energy of mindfulness in order to receive the collective energy of the sangha, you will have a powerful source of energy for your transformation and healing."[11]

The Wacuri Method

The purpose of this book is to expand the practice of social meditation for the world. The Wacuri Method of meditation is innovative and interactive — creating a collective experience of powerful transmission through meditative practice, as well as shared space which allows for nurturance, connectivity and insight as a result of the group experience. The Wacuri Method allows for the best vs. worst use of technology — instead of providing a digital platform that creates disconnection, social isolation and competition, it brings like-hearted individuals together in collective meditation practice — allowing for the experience of Inter-Being across the digital plane.

The aim of the Wacuri Method is to make it almost effortless to connect deeply with yourself, others and the universe. Curious.live is an experimental online platform that enables people to make deep

---

[11] Thich Nhat Hanh. (2017, July). Retrieved from https://www.lionsroar.com/the-practice-of-sangha

connections quickly and easily through five-minute guided journeys followed by sharing their experiences and discoveries. A journey seeks to give you an intimate connection to something and awaken a sense of awe and curiosity from that thing, which could be an object like the sun, a feeling like love, or an idea like living fully in the moment. You and a friend or new acquaintances journey together, and your experience strengthens their experience, just as theirs strengthens yours. The African proverb reminds us, when we want to go fast, we go alone — and when we want to go far, we go together. Wacuri has developed a program that can help us to go fast, and go far. By going together in brief journeys, we begin to experience that all is interconnected.

At the heart of the Wacuri Method is the recognition that deeper connections make for stronger societies. During a Wacuri Journey, connections are forged in an intentional way within the group biofield. The connections are then enhanced and deepened through sharing moments of awe. This shared interaction promotes relational intelligence, adaptability, and flexible thinking.

If you are reading this book, quite likely you are among the millions of people who are part of the movement toward conscious awakening. You may even be offering your skills and expertise to those around you to better their own path of growth, health and fulfillment. You may be or hope to be a personal growth practitioner, a yoga instructor, meditation teacher, healer, therapist or a coach, dedicated to waking up and helping others do the same.

If you look closely, in our bodies, in our cells, in our relationships, in the stars, in the entire cosmos, all is eternal movement and change. The most adaptive way to surf the changes is to stay curious, and stay connected. This book is an invitation to the intuitive, magical, inventive, capable you—the you that is everything and everyone—connected with all your relations and all life here and throughout time. May you further your enjoyment of the experience of InterBeing throughout your human journey.

Dr. Shamini Jain, Founder and CEO of the Consciousness and Healing Initiative (CHI)

CHAPTER ONE

WHY WAKE UP CURIOUS?

"We are all equal beings and the universe is our relations with each other."

~ Thaddeus Golas,
The Lazy Man's Guide to Enlightenment

First published in 1971, Thaddeus Golas' cult classic, The Lazy Man's Guide to Enlightenment posits the notion that "enlightenment doesn't care how you get there." A blend of the spiritual and the ontological folded into a base of traditional physics, Golas' book has been in print ever since. It ranks quite high in Amazon sales ratings for a book that gets no promotion whatsoever. The title alone is likely sufficient to trigger any number of one-click impulse-buys. But most of us would never be deeply satisfied if we were truly lazy. As a species, we're just too darn curious to settle into laziness as a lifestyle choice.

The burgeoning field of neuroscience is daily altering our view of what we are and what we can be. In light of the remarkable new perspectives we will review in this book, we propose a far more fulfilling, even exhilarating, alternative: The Curious Person's Guide to Enlightenment.

Power Flows Into the Moment

Why curious? Because we all know the power of "Be Here Now" and curiosity, unlike any other human quality, has the power to immediately refresh your NOW.

The moment you get curious, power flows into the moment. You're simply with what's so. Only when you are truly present with what is, can you feel into what's truly wondrous about life's many ups and downs. Then you can reach for what's finer, while holding the dynamic tension between what is and what's wanted. From there, you can lean into love and shoot your arrow of intent toward the future of your choice rather than react to what is off-kilter in the moment. And we all know there is plenty that falls into the off-kilter category on an everyday basis.

Just look around. You'd have to be half dead not to be upset about the state of our world. But "upset" is a sub-optimal state of mind for what is most needed in our world today: effective collaboration and creative problem solving.

In this sense, "Wake Up Curious" is meant to be a rally cry for a better tomorrow. It's about waking up in the morning to greet the day in a new way. It's about waking up moment to moment and directing your attention to what is already present rather than to what is missing or needed. It's about waking up to the truth of who you truly are.

When you wake up curious, your natural desires come online in a whole new way. Your wants become a source of inspiration rather than frustration. Your needs become a guiding light. And your longings become a friend instead of a source of pain. You stand in a pristine place, free from the past, open to flow. In that fresh wanting, you can relax and let go.

This is what's most needed in a world where so many feel so alone and isolated. Where so-called "connectivity" is at an all-time high, while feelings of loneliness and isolation have never been more all-pervasive. Where social media gives the impression of connecting with others in a meaningful way but, in reality, we are often left feeling more alone at the end of the day.

The Root of All Neurosis

Human relations are the stuff of existence. Without each other, we cease to exist. There's a reason the root of all neurosis is the fear of rejection, or sense that we are isolated and alone. Without "our tribe" few of us would survive. To be shunned is to be banished from the flock and left to die. Just as the fear of snakes is hardwired into every human brain, the fear that comes with feeling disconnected and isolated is REAL. It has a biological basis and evolutionary underpinning. You can't escape it and no amount of identity politics will resolve the deeply human need to belong.

Belonging. It's at the very base of Maslow's hierarchy of needs. Still and yet, our relations with our fellow human beings are rife with challenges. We experience ourselves as separate and thus feel out of place. We propose that the experience of separation is an illusion, one that often haunts us until we die. Oddly enough, it is in death that most of us discover that we are, in fact, one with everything. And we also discover that the very concepts of where and when are merely a dream of separateness.

Endlessly Creative Consciousness

Like our relationships with each other, our relationship to the biosphere is tragically out of sync. A life lived on overdrive makes it very difficult to feel the earthly rhythms our very nature depends on for its humanness. Look closely at what's really going on. Any thinking person would have to conclude that our species is playing a dangerous game of chicken with its own extinction.

Still and yet, there is plenty of good news. Look closely again and you'll see the eternal verities — beauty, goodness, and truth — alive and well. Pockets of peace are everywhere apparent. The human spirit is reaching for the stars. More and more, we are turning the other cheek in reverence for our Universal Human Rights. More and more, everyday people are stepping into a heroic role. More and more, humans are discovering what it means to behave impeccably. And more and more, we are realizing the dynamic whole of which we are a part. Ours is an endlessly creative consciousness, an intelligent life form with potential far beyond what we have accomplished, or failed to accomplish, thus far.

Will we follow the apocalyptic trajectory of "the ending times" and nosedive our global civilization like the naysayers proclaim? Or will we pull up out of the decent and point our nose toward a more coherent, stable future? Is it even possible to stop the downward momentum?

Nobody knows. All we know is that we're not dead yet.

We also know that mindfulness and meditation is catching on. We know the insights of mystics and poets are evermore relevant in challenging times. We know the words of wisdom teachers are full of grace. We know we are waking up to our agency and realizing that our state of oneness gives us more than Universal Human Rights, but also Universal Human Responsibilities. Many of us also know that the human race is in desperate need of a divine intervention—a bigger picture perspective that takes us beyond what we know now and into the possible. And we're in dire need of skillful means to act on whatever it is that gets revealed when we pray "Thy will, not mine be done."

A Breakthrough Method

In the pages that follow, you will discover a breakthrough method—a skillful means to get connected and stay connected. Like so many breakthroughs, this one came about out of necessity, not because someone had a big idea or set out to invent the latest and greatest whatever. It came about because of one person's urgent plea. One person's desire to tap into the wisdom anyone can access by making a conscious choice to expand their awareness. And to be able to accomplish that even when one has a busy schedule and a mere five minutes to spare.

Across this beautiful blue-green planet, people are waking up to an inner quiet, a place of pure witness where they can find peace — even in the midst of catastrophic uncertainty and unrelenting pain. Meditation gives us wiggle room around the "sky is falling" compression chamber inside our head. It helps us let go of our petty egoic resistance and embrace the miracles all around us. When your internal dialog turns into an assault rifle, a moment of pure presence can click the safety on. When the external world kicks up a fuss, creates a ruckus, or turns into mayhem, the person who has access to inner stillness and calm can experience what most would call "insanity" as pure energy. To be fully present and alert is the ultimate challenge and the direct path to conscious awakening. The admonishment to relinquish the past and put your faith in the future may seem like madness, but the alternative is truly insane.

It has been asserted that we are destined to know the dark beyond the stars before we comprehend the nature of our own journey. That may be true in the first attention in terms of language, thinking and the assignment of meaning to all things. But by being fully present we awaken to our true nature. We find a direct path to consciousness writ large. We awaken to a state of knowing beyond intellect, beyond the information channelled to the hippocampus and stored in the brain in synapses. We exchange our analytical approach to life for self-knowledge, and wake up to a place of pure witness where we can find peace.

Let us breathe together, put all our relations on the altar of our deepest intent, and envision a friendly and collaborative universe. Let us remember "being green again" and share a moment of awe. Let us develop relational intelligence and invite ourselves and those we care for into an era of wonder. Let us embrace the good, the true, and the beautiful, while refusing to ignore the horrible, ugly, nasty aspects of reality. And let us move through these uber-challenging, difficult times with curiosity as our wilderness guide.

The universe is ever-evolving. Nothing about the human mind and life itself is static, and nothing about who you are is finite. As Buckminster Fuller famously said, "I appear to be a verb." You are not an object and yet, to a large degree, you have been objectified. To be sure, that objectification has made you smaller than you are. This book is an invitation to the bigger you, the curious you, the intuitive, magical, inventive, capable you, the you that is everything and everyone—connected with all your relations and all life here and throughout time.

Welcome to the sphere of your Infinite Being. Welcome home.

CHAPTER TWO

FLOW IS A DEEPER CONNECTION

"When I was a very young man, I somehow found myself in dialogue with trees. I would go to them for comfort as a young boy, very young, like five, or seven. I would feel as if they were talking to me and giving me guidance."

~ Dan Spinner

Dan Spinner's father was materialist, a scientist with a Ph.D. in Chemical Engineering. When Dan was seven years old, he went to his dad and asked, "Dad, do you talk to trees too?"

His father cocked his head slightly and asked, "What did you say?"

"Do you talk to trees?"

"Don't talk about that," his dad said. "That's nonsense. I don't want to hear you talk like that ever again."

Dan was thunderstruck. Here he'd thought his dad knew everything. He was his father, for gosh sakes!

It was a marker moment for Dan. A moment when he realized, like all children do, that his father didn't have all the answers. He knew something his father didn't.

Ever since he was very young, Dan had talked to trees. More than that, he had conversations with trees. As a very young boy, he would turn to the trees when he was upset. The trees, in turn, would comfort and guide him. They were his friends. And he wasn't about to stop talking to trees.

It was the beginning of a compelling need — what could even be called a mandate from Dan's soul — to question any authority other than his own experience. Thus possessed of inner authority from an early age, Dan learned that outer authorities are often misinformed, and conventional wisdom is often vastly overrated. Sound familiar?

Encounters With the Natural World

As far back as he can remember, Dan had a relationship with the trees. That relationship segued to the wind and, eventually, to the entire natural world. "The wind would respond when I needed solace," Dan recalls. "I would feel it rise up. It was all very alive and totally interactive. And the communication was far from one-way."

As a boy and throughout his teens, Dan would turn to the wind or the trees whenever he felt confused or agitated. Nature was his familiar. The natural world would respond to him—not in language, but in feelings. This is how he came to understand interchange and energetic flow. He didn't have a vocabulary for it at the time, but that didn't matter.

"The experience was just so wonderful," he recalls. "And it got stronger and stronger and stronger over time. I remember one long car trip in our old Nash Rambler. We were going camping to the Thousand Islands near the St. Lawrence River. Dad was driving, Mom was in the front seat looking at maps, and I was in the back seat. I remember looking out the window and soaking up the entire landscape. I didn't have words for it then, but I was experiencing the countryside energetically. It put me into a reverie. I was completely outside of time. My body was in the car, but my awareness was soaring across the land."

When Dan reflected on the experience, he found it quite curious. Not surprising. The world he was encountering so vividly did not match the world he'd been taught was real and solid. The material world of form was somehow separate from the world of his lived experience. From a very young age, profound experiences like these left deep impressions on his mind, his body, and his awareness.

Alternate-reality experiences like Dan's encounters with the natural world are fairly common among children prior to age five. They tend to taper off once a child goes to kindergarten and all but disappear once they start grammar school. But Dan wasn't like most children. He never abandoned his alternate-reality and never stopped talking to the trees.

The Truth Behind the Word

"There was this story about reality — or so-called reality," Dan recalls, "and then there was me, always questioning, 'What? That doesn't make any sense.' It was more than an issue of internal or external authority. It was clear to me there was an avoided reality behind much of what was assumed to be true.

I just knew that what my father and other authority figures were presenting to my schoolmates and me as given (i.e.: factual) wasn't necessarily the whole story. Especially confusing were the instances when the supposed given was about matters of importance.

Dan learned to live with that ambiguity. By the time he was 13, he'd become that kid who had to get down to the real truth. No matter the topic, he wanted to know the bottom line.

"I had an insatiable curiosity," Dan says. "It got me in trouble. My family went to an Episcopalian church in a suburb outside Toronto. Like a lot of Christian denominations, Episcopalians send their kids to Sunday school until they're thirteen. At thirteen, you get confirmed and then you get to join the entire congregation on Sunday morning. Well, when I was in Sunday school, the only thing that caught my interest was this guy named Jesus. I now know that I could feel his energy but, as a kid, all I knew was that I had a hundred questions about him. Why did he do that? Why didn't he do that? Why this? Why not that?"

Dan was unrelenting. He would hijack the Sunday school lesson plan with his questions. The teacher often had no answers. Finally, she tired of his questions and said, "You know what Danny? You actually can't ask questions in Sunday School."

Danny said, "Really? When can I ask questions?"

"You can ask questions when you get confirmed and join the congregation in church."

"Okay, fine," Danny said. So he started writing out his questions. He had a notebook full of questions scribbled down in his prepubescent cursive.

He turned 13, got confirmed, and joined the congregation for the Sunday service for the first time.

Sitting in the church pew in the second row, he stuck up his hand. His father gave him a stern look, leaned over, and said, "What are you doing?"

Danny said, "I'm asking a question."

"You can't ask questions in church," his father scolded.

Danny said, "Man! They lied to me." He got up and walked out of the church.

Dan didn't walk out of that church because they lied to him. He walked out because his curiosity was unwelcome. He had a profound realization that day: authority figures and so-called wisdom teachers wouldn't be able to help him uncover the truth behind the words. They wouldn't be able to lead him to the true reality.

He would have to find it on his own.

The Way of Harmony

It was the early 60s. A British philosopher by the name of Alan Watts had published a book titled The Way of Zen and quickly became a key voice for a new generation of seekers. Keenly interested in Eastern thought and hungry for a deep spiritual identity, these hopefuls began to swarm around Watts.

When Dan stumbled across The Way of Zen, his mind was blown. The poems held the exact same energy of the trees he had been talking to his whole life. Likewise the guy named Jesus he'd heard about in Sunday school. Thus began Dan's intellectual spiritual awakening.

Previously, Dan had only taken passive notice of the similarity between what he felt with the trees and what he felt about Jesus. He'd wondered, "How can that be?" and lived with the question on a subliminal level for a number of years. With the sudden realization, "Oh, it's the energy that's the same!" his mental frame aligned with his lived experience. Up until this point, his awakening had been at a visceral level that was primarily kinesthetic and non-verbal. His intellect hadn't been involved, but now it was.

Sound familiar? Not surprising. That's essentially how awakening works. The energetic feeling comes first; the mental frame for the experience is secondary. You have likely had that experience yourself. You may be having it now.

Flash forward to about six years later. Dan is in college when some guardian angel grabs him by the scruff of the neck and pulls him into a particular Aikido dojo. Dan didn't have much interest in martial arts. He was a bit of a jock, loved gymnastics, played hockey, and had been on the wrestling team. Somewhere along the line he'd read an article about Aikido that caught his attention. A particular phrase, the way of harmony, had stuck in his mind. So he sat down on the wooden bench along the wall of the dojo to observe the class.

He was gobsmacked. A small Japanese-Canadian man, "Sensei" the students called him, was moving like the wind. He fought, but hurt no-one. And he never got injured.

Oh, my God, Dan thought. It feels like the trees.

He had entered an alternative universe.

Coincidentally, that dojo was five minutes from Dan's apartment near the University of Toronto where he was attending college. He went back a week later and watched again. He thought, I don't know what that is, but I want it.

He studied with that Sensei for the next 10 years. Two nights a week, he attended class, no matter what. Even after he moved to London Ontario more than 100 miles away, he continued to attend twice-weekly classes. That's how much he wanted what his teacher had. What Dan didn't know when he began training, but saw as priceless down the road, was that his Sensei had studied with the founder of Aikido in Tokyo.

In the subtle, internal martial arts such as tai chi, qigong, hsing-i and bagua—all of which are lineage traditions—studying with a master is mission critical if you want the deeper teaching. The "truth behind the words" cannot be delivered through words and physical exercises, only through transmission. Dan thought, I wonder if transmission can be experienced and shared by everyone all the time? This was his first instinctive move toward the democratization of spirituality. In fact it was the very loneliness of Dan's spiritual journey that became his driving motivation to address this common experience and look for solutions to this human existential dilemma.

Higher Order Information-Sharing

Receiving transmission is a bit of a mystery — until you experience it. Truth be told, we all receive transmissions all the time, we're just not aware of it. Not all transmissions are profound, knee-buckling realizations from the Universe. If you've ever had one, you know the score: it's unforgettable. A powerful transmission can be a life-shaping experience that changes absolutely everything.

The Universe isn't always selective when it delivers these revelations, doesn't seem to care if you're a wizard or a Muggle. So far, nobody has ascertained just how or why certain individuals become the "designated recipient" (for lack of a simpler term) of certain transmissions. Sure, the Buddha was a prince before he sat under the tree, but Byron Katie got enlightened and she wasn't royalty. She was an overweight, unhappy housewife with a drinking problem. So why would she be the one to receive the powerful transmission that led to her permanent awakening and a worldwide following? Nobody knows.

All we can say for sure is that certain people receive a spontaneous transmission from the Universe in a certain way, at a certain time, in a certain place. Some of those people go on to write books, others create religious groups, establish mystery schools, or sell their wares online. Often, they are outright compelled to do so, and their inner being won't let them rest until they do. Other recipients of Universal Truth simply walk around happier than most, saying little of their realization, just going about their business and doing good works. And while they may appear to be doing such works "out of the goodness of their heart," what's also true is that the inner freedom they enjoy gives them abundant energy for helping others along the way.

There's a remarkable quality to these revelatory insights and the sense of freedom enjoyed by people who have them. Once the new reality is registered, it can be actualized and established in a being as reality. In time it can become their "new normal." The process by which this occurs is unique to each person. It yields what seems to be a standing wave of energy, a human being that feels as if they are vibrating at a higher frequency. That frequency can be transferred, as energy, from one person to another, as in the classic teacher-student relationship. This is what is known as transmission. Energetic transmission is, in essence, supra-conceptual and supra-physical information sharing. In the ancient traditions, Taoism for example, the information is received by the student as a body of knowledge, whole and complete in itself. However, it can only be integrated, made real, and put to practical use over time and with practice. Metaphorically speaking, we could say the body of knowledge gets transferred from soul to soul, but it takes what it takes for the personality to understand and cultivate its use in everyday life. This takes practice, of course. Fortunately, the rewards tend to be tangible, making it easier to move toward a new way of being in the world.

In the Flow

Dan's teacher learned Aikido from Morihei Ueshiba, the founder of Aikido. Often called O' Sensei (meaning "Old Teacher"), Ueshiba, taught via transmission, the way his Sensei had taught him. His Sensei wasn't an educated man and didn't have a lot of sophistication, spiritually speaking, but he could move like the wind in total harmony. Yes, he could protect himself. And yes, he was rolling around and moving this way and that. Plenty of motion, but all within the discipline of centering that is at the heart of Aikido.

Imagine for a moment that you're a stubborn 19 year old and this little Japanese guy, four inches shorter and 40 pounds lighter than you, grabs your wrist and says, "Move. Move." You push, but you can't move him. You can't even move your own body.

"Move!" he says.

You try again. He won't budge. And your own body is no longer obeying your commands. You're much bigger and considerably younger than this guy, but even with all your physical strength, you can't move him at all.

"Move!" he says again.

You can't. With steam coming out of every orifice in your body, you wonder, "What is this guy talking about?"

That's what happened to Dan. It would reveal itself slowly over a decade as he realized that his teacher was taking him to a very different place — a dimension outside the ordinary realm of what we think of as physics.

The way of harmony, whether in an Aikido dojo or in the dojo of life, consists of many important revelatory moments and many essential teachings. In Aikido, a cornerstone teaching is the experience of being in your center. First the Aikidoist learns to find their center, then to project their ki or life force energy out in front of them. It sounds more esoteric than it is. Centering is surprisingly easy. And while projecting your energy requires a bit of training, it is relatively simple to learn and eminently practical.

Finding your center is really a process of realizing you have an energy field and registering the fact that it's all around you. In contrast, projecting your energy from that center is the process of generating that energy field with a clear intent to create a safety bubble of sorts. That bubble then interacts with another person's energy field. In Aikido, you actually do the various moves at the boundary of those energy interactions.

Again, it sounds more esoteric than it is. These energy interactions happen all the time in everyday life.

Say you're at your favorite java joint enjoying a mocha latte when someone with a bad attitude walks into the place. You don't know the person, and you don't pay them much attention, but you sense their negativity. You just feel it. In fact, you can't help but register the "bad vibes" they throw off. Not surprising, then, when they make some rude or off-color comment, confirming the hit you got when they walked in. Their emotional state hits you before they even open their mouth. You were interacting with their biofield.

Dr. Shamini Jain, CEO of the Consciousness and Healing Initiative defines the biofield as "subtle energies that regulate health and emotions." It includes the energy fields (sometimes called auras) around the human body. As early as the first century BCE, both Tibetan and Vedic traditions have been discussing biofield interactions in terms specific to their understanding of the phenomenon.

In Aikido, this phenomenon is known as the ki field (chi field in qigong), and the Aikidoist interacts with this biofield in a very purposeful way. With the center positioned in front of the body and projected to those around, the Aikidoist can remain in a flow state when attacked. Rather than reflexively defend, or reactively counter-attack, there's just flow. In this state, the body just knows how to move. And it does, beautifully so.

That is what Dan witnessed the first day he entered the dojo. A man in a state of flow. A state he would eventually practice for his entire adult life and learn to share with others. Dan was beginning to glimpse that a "shared flow" was infectious and invoked a shared resonance between people. Years later, this understanding became the core of the Wacuri Method.

Harmony Is Our Natural State

What gives the Aikidoist access to the flow state is simple (but not easy): they have discovered what it is to be completely present in their physical bodies. Notice the choice of words here: "have discovered what it is to be present" is very different than "has learned to be in the present." That discovery, along with a growing understanding of centering, allows the Aikidoist to become aware of their own energy field. Ultimately, an individual who is aware of their own energy field can develop agency in the biofield. Once we understand the nature of the shared biofield, we have access to a high flow state where the interactions with another's biofield are felt or seen. In this way, two or more people can find themselves in a harmonious, elegant dance.

We have this notion that the present is a place. It tracks back to Ram Dass and Be Here Now. The notion that we can be located in the here and now has been advanced in such a way as to hone our attention, but the notion falls short of clarifying our intent. In that sense, it's something of a ruse, a subtle misdirect. Discovering what it is to be present is essentially discovering how to get out of your own way. When one is truly present, the mind and ego have ceased their incessant mind chatter and layering-on of interpretations and assumptions about what is occurring in front of you. Rather than "be here now" or be fully in the present moment, the state of flow is one wherein you lose yourself altogether.

Former head of the Department of Psychology at the University of Chicago, Mihaly Csíkszentmihályi devoted much of his career to investigating the optimal experience of flow. Known as the architect of the state of flow, Csíkszentmihályi named, studied, and has been writing about this common, yet elusive condition of mind and body since the mid 70s. His seminal work, Flow: The Psychology of Optimal Experience summarizes a lifetime of work by advancing his theory that humans feel the happiest when they are completely absorbed in some activity.

Have you ever been engaged in a challenging endeavor and fallen into a reverie that is all-consuming and intrinsically pleasurable? Be it coding or snowboarding, playing basketball or Texas Hold 'em, writing or painting or playing guitar, your everyday self seems to disappear into the activity. In a state of deep concentration, we can become so absorbed in what we are pursuing—be it a physical, mental, emotional, or spiritual endeavor—all else seems to disappear. In this state of flow, only that which is commanding our full attention seems to matter. Granted, the larger reality may intrude if, say, a child screams or a spouse barges into the room. But while in the state of flow, the larger reality of life, along with time and other responsibilities, fade into the background for awhile. In flow, you may even lose track of time altogether. Completely unaware of how many hours have passed, you might suddenly realize that you haven't eaten all day, or that you've been up all night and the sun is about to come up.

Characterized by intrinsic motivation, this state of full-on engagement finds us, in Csíkszentmihályi's words, "completely involved in an activity for its own sake. The ego falls away. Time flies. Every action, movement, and thought follows inevitably from the previous one, like playing jazz. Your whole being is involved, and you're using your skills to the utmost."

What is it that allows us to access this delicious state of full absorption? We achieve a state of flow when an activity fulfills two criteria simultaneously. First, the activity needs to be a match for our skills. Secondly, the challenge at hand should test those skills and, in the best case scenario, push us beyond our previous level to greater mastery of those skills.

Moreover, according to Csikszentmihályi, some combination of the following will be present when we are induced into a flow state:

- Action and awareness merge into a seamless whole.
- We have clarity about specific goals.
- There is an immediate and unambiguous feedback loop built into the activity.
- The task at hand requires concentration.
- We're simultaneously in control and required to surrender.
- Time is transformed.
- We lose self-consciousness.
- The activity is intrinsically rewarding.

It's tempting to believe that optimal experience of this nature occurs by chance or coincidence simply because, at times, it does. What's less obvious and more to the point in our exploration, the state of flow more often occurs during structured activity. Which brings us back to Dan and a key lesson he learned in the dojo.

Learn To Play With Life Force Energy

Dan will never forget that moment during a class when his entire world took on a new dimension.

He had begun to speak, addressing his teacher in the usual way, "Sensei..." when his teacher casually cut him off and said, "Don't call me Sensei. Call me Henry."

Dan paused, not quite understanding, then continued, "Henry, I think you're telling me that you want me to head directly into the most fearful place I have with my intention and energy."

His teacher replied, "That's exactly what I'm telling you to do."

Oh my God, Dan thought. Then he said aloud, "I don't know if I can do that, but now I understand what you're asking me to do."

Imagine for a moment, a six foot four black belt giant of a man comes at you on the attack. If you're not familiar with your deepest fear-place, you won't be able to be totally centered, present and aware of what's occurring. On the other hand, if you've made friends with that place of fear by leaning into it instead of reflexively avoiding it, you can stay in your center and your place of highest flow, while feeling the fear.

Fast forward to 1991. Dan had been looking for a meditation practice for a number of years. He wanted to find an approach to meditation that matched his Aikido practice. Over the course of a decade, he tried about eight different forms of meditation. Finally, he found an energy body approach in which the all-important "center" was identical to the center he'd found in the dojo. And while Aikido was an Eastern practice, this energy body approach was from a Western European/Egyptian philosophical tradition. When the two came together, Dan once again heard a thunderclap.

You have probably had your own series of thunderclaps. These sequential, sometimes accidental, always interrelated, "Ah-ha!" moments run through your body as a whole new level of awareness dawns. It's as if some part of you that's been asleep suddenly wakes up. Generally, this occurs in the body first; the intellect follows.

For Dan Spinner, experimenting with the flow of ki (the Japanese word for chi), translated into his work in the nonprofit and business world. He wanted to be in flow both in and out of the dojo so he started experimenting while in meetings. It took years of Forrest-Gumping his way through, meditating, learning to play with life force energy, working with his energy body and the energy fields that surround us in everyday life. The process of integrating the innumerable lessons into his professional activities became Dan's vocation, leading to a very successful career in the nonprofit and business sectors. He has used the principles outlined in this book to which have helped him raise hundreds of millions of dollars. In addition, he has served as senior leader, Vice President, or CEO for a number of for-profit organizations, universities, and hospitals including the University of British Columbia and Oshawa General Hospital and the Deepak Chopra Foundation. He has acted as Strategic Advisor to many enterprises, started and ran numerous businesses including The Omega Center Bookstore and Wacuri. Inc.

Nowadays Dan is totally comfortable admitting that, in his words, "I still don't really know what I'm doing, but now I am totally comfortable with not knowing. In fact, I welcome not knowing as an open invitation to the discovery I know it to be."

Get Cozy With Not Knowing

In our estimation, the need to know what you're doing at the personality level is one of the primary blocks to awakening. What we most want you to hear is this: you don't actually need to know anything. Your ego wants desperately to know, but the less you know the better when it comes to the process of awakening. You're going to discover that you're not who you thought you were at all. In time, you will be able to discern various levels of your existence that are both invisible and inaccessible to the ego-dominated self. You'll be able to navigate back and forth between and beyond a variety of existential domains. It's a fascinating study and it's not at all hard to handle and eventually master when you are doing so consciously.

Along the way, you will have any number of thunderclap moments. Wake Up Curious and you are sure to be thunderstruck again and again. The Wacuri Method is just one way—a very particular and accessible way—to exercise new muscles that get you to the center of everything. The method quickly takes you IN so you can go OUT. Rather than spend twenty years in a monastery, you might find yourself connected to the vastness of the Universe in no time at all.

It's worth noting that we did not set out to develop a method. Quite the contrary. The method grew out of one person's need. What began as a discovery process started to take shape in a distinct sequence or, to use a term from fiction writing, as a series of "beats." This sequence or pattern was only identified in hindsight. It emerged organically over time. Dan Spinner says, "Calling it a method makes it sound much more deliberate than the process has been. I have never gone into a journey trying to create a moment of awe, nor do I think in terms of seven stages. Only when Rob Read joined the group and noted that there was a rhythm and a sequence did it dawn on us that a pattern had emerged. That pattern was subsequently adopted as a method. But the process was anything but deliberate and methodical, rather it was emergent.

The word "method" is contrary to the spontaneity and flow characteristic of Wacuri journeys. We now have a taxonomy of journeys, 350 of them at the time of this writing. Most of them fall into readily identifiable categories: nature, healing, space, etc. But none of us planned this or identified categories at the outset; they just happened as part of an iterative discovery process. It's a bit like making love. You can learn a method and pick up techniques, but when the moment comes, you have to let go of all that and be in flow.

Regardless of whether it's called a method or a mind-meld, a shamanic practice or a guided visualization, the journey process brings ancient traditions alive. It blends Eastern energy arts, philosophical traditions, theosophy, modern spiritual technology, and Light Body meditation, into a practical, actionable form that is experienced in the presence of others. The aim is for you to be able to wake up and stay awake in relationships. To reclaim your essential energy, your vitality, your heart, and your mind. To drop needless burdens so you are free to take up the very real challenges of life in these expansive and yet terrifying times — whether you are alone or in the presence of another person.

CHAPTER THREE

SEEING THINGS INTO EXISTENCE

Born in July of 1939 while Austria was under Nazi rule, Ingrid Winter was a "runt." The attending obstetrician, one Doctor Richter, told her parents that "in the spirit of National Socialism" such children were not permitted to live. He moved her into a closet with no authorized feedings and left her to die. His rationale—that she was unworthy of the Aryan race and therefore expendable—is the kind of insanity one might expect in a totalitarian regime. Thinking for oneself is expressly prohibited in such a milieu.

Ingrid's parents, like most Austrians, had been passive during the German takeover of their country. But this was personal. And horrifying. The teeny 7-month old preemie wasn't a runt, she was their daughter. Compliance was out of the question. They were not about to stand by and let their child be killed by the Nazi machine.

Ingrid's father, Heinrich Winter, went from one official to the next, asking for Doctor Richter's order to be rescinded. After two days of political paperwork and approvals, Ingrid's parents were able to retrieve their infant daughter from the closet where she had been left, completely abandoned and on her own. By then a jaundiced skeleton, Ingrid was transferred to the neonatal pediatric unit where she was cared for over the next several weeks.

Then, on September 1, Hitler marched into Poland. World War II began two days later. Ingrid's father, a Ph.D. Meteorologist, was immediately drafted by the Nazi military machine.

The Natural Inclination of Mind

Most people have little memory of their earliest years, but Ingrid wasn't like most people when she grew up. She had visual memories of her surroundings from the time she was in the crib. Had her time in the closet made her more alert than the typical neonate? Had the natural inclination of mind to stay alert and encode various patterns of sight and sound been sped up, even honed, by her innate instinct for survival? Had this experience not only saved her life, but lent her unusual capacities?

No one can say for sure, but it's a curious question.

What we do know for sure is that Ingrid grew up in wartime. Dr. Winter was a meteorologist in the German Air Force. The family, along with the entire flight advisory weather service, lived in the castle Schloß Freiling in the village of Oftering. Schloß Freiling had once been a medieval manor. Ingrid had detailed memories of both the interior and grounds around the castle, as well as the grownups who inhabited it. She was a sickly child, but that did not stop her mind from growing strong. She had a curious mind and studied quite a lot. By the time she was six, she could read novels in English.

As an adult, Ingrid was an academic and a member of the progressive Catholic Church. She moved to the US, married William Thomas Poole, and was living in Oklahoma with her husband and two children, Henry and Irene. She believed in science, women's rights, and rights for gay people. According to the story Henry grew up with, the ultra-conservative Oklahoma governor came up with a plan to deal with an emerging social problem: hippies. As the story went, the governor rallied the legislature to build a Liberal Arts core education program at a flea-bitten, Nowheresville college. Supposedly, the governor couldn't care less about the Liberal Arts, but it would serve as a honey pot to attract all the hippies and, presumably, keep them out of the better universities or, at the very least, out of his hair.

That's how Ingrid became a college professor—at least, that's what Henry grew up believing. As it turns out this story wasn't quite true, but the tale had power nonetheless and served an important purpose in Henry's development.

In any case, the university hired Ingrid, along with other out-of-the-box thinkers to teach art, philosophy, and religion. Ingrid and her colleagues taught one of the nation's first interdisciplinary studies programs. She taught 15th century art in big lecture halls. The faculty would watch films and listen to Janis Joplin with the students. Such activities were unheard of at more conservative colleges.

A Free-thinking Household

Ingrid's 4,000 square foot home two blocks from campus became a meeting place for college students—some even ended up living there. The house was full of conversation and argument. Math, science, history, religion, art; these were the topics discussed around the Poole house.

"Growing up with free-thinking parents in a free-thinking household in Oklahoma of all places... it was definitely formative," says Henry Poole. "Like the time my Dad played a trick on the preacher to get him to leave our family alone."

Son of a Presbyterian Evangelist, Henry Poole's father had been born and raised in Oklahoma. After military service, he went to seminary to become a preacher like his dad. "But my dad had a photographic memory," Henry recalls. "He studied the Bible at length. Once he started seeing the inconsistencies, he looked into how the Bible was translated. The basic flaws in the text led him to dismiss it as utter nonsense. My mother believed that there was a higher purpose behind it and held her ground. She had this great love for Jesus that kept her faith alive. But my dad wasn't having any of it. He became an atheist."

Still and yet, the preacher showed up at the Poole family home to talk with Tom Poole every Sunday. Southern Baptist ministers could be quite tenacious. "The man was a racist," Henry recalls. "In those days, Southern Baptists taught that black people were black because God had burned them because they were an evil race. It was ridiculous."

On several occasions, Tom Poole told the preacher, with requisite Southern politeness, that he wasn't interested in going to his church. But the preacher kept coming over. Tired of the preacher's Sunday visits, Henry's father devised a plan to get rid of the man. And while Henry doesn't have a clear memory of the event himself, the story became the stuff of family legend.

"I must've been about four, my sister was probably six," Henry explains. "We often ran out of the house naked because, well… that's just what Germans do. For Europeans, it's not a big deal. Then one day, my dad gave us special instructions on what to do next time the preacher came to the house, saying, 'Next time he comes over, I'll go sit down with him in the living room…'"

A big, beautiful Southern mansion with granite pillars and beamed ceiling, the Poole family home had a huge living room at the front of the house. Just inside the wide front door there was a library on the right side with a big leather couch facing into the foyer. Opposite that, on the other side of the expansive entryway, was a sitting room that spilled into the large living room. From the sitting room, one could see into the library. Henry's father told his children, "When I sit down and start talking to the preacher, I want you and your sister to get on that couch and pretend like you're making out."

Henry and his sister weren't always the most obedient children, but this sounded like fun so they did as they were told — or so the story goes.

"The priest comes in and sits down," Henry explains. "My father was talking to him; we're running around, butt-naked, jumping on the couch, kissing and rubbing each other, pretending like we're playing with each other. The preacher never came back."

Visualizing Results

Henry's uncle had also started down the path to become a preacher but changed direction and became a businessman — and a very successful businessman at that. Starting in the 60s, he was involved in developing golf courses. First as General Manager, then as Executive Vice President of ClubCorp, he played a lead role in building the largest golf club enterprise in the world.

"The country clubs in Dallas were for the elite," said Richard Poole, who joined ClubCorp in 1960 and retired from his Executive VP position in 2017. "The idea was that there was a built-in market of mobile and upwardly mobile families who wanted to play golf at affordable prices."

ClubCorp didn't adopt the exclusionary practices that were common then. They put Jews, women and eventually blacks on the clubs' boards. In his book, *The King of Clubs*, ClubCorp's CEO, Robert Dedman writes: "Race, gender or religion didn't make any difference to us."

Over the years, ClubCorp became a global company with $1.6 billion in assets. It opened its first business club in a Dallas skyscraper in 1962. A real estate division came on line in 1976. The first foreign property, a city club, opened in Taipei, Taiwan, in 1982.

Always an admirer of his uncle's success, Henry talked with him about meditation one afternoon. He was in his early thirties at the time and had been meditating for about ten years. He was visiting his dad, who was undergoing cancer treatment. Henry traveled to Tulsa, Oklahoma to visit his father. His dad's brother had also come to visit. When the two men went out to lunch, Henry told his uncle about his meditation practice.

"I do these visualizations," he explained. "I sit quietly and conjure a detailed image of things I want in my mind."

"Oh, I've been doing that since the '60s," his uncle replied.

"Really?" Henry asked. He was astonished. He'd always thought of his uncle as quite conservative.

"Yes. If we had a negotiation or important business transaction, I'd get together with a couple people on my team before the meeting," his uncle explained. "We would clear our thoughts then go through this process of imagining the outcome we wanted. Then we would go into the meeting and conduct the business at hand. We had an 80% success rate."

Henry remembers his uncle emphasizing the fact that they never told anybody about what they were doing. "They were building country clubs, for heaven's sake" he said. "Their business associates were bigwigs from oil, steel, and automotive industries, conservative business sectors where you didn't talk about such things. But my uncle and his team were essentially meditating together to give themselves a leg-up during big meetings. I'm sitting there, eating a burger with a man who's on the board of a multi-billion dollar business and he's telling me this is a secret to his success. That left a big impression on me."

Henry became all the more interested in personal and group meditation and its practical applications. Like many of his cohort, his meditation practice was self-styled. He'd experimented a bit, mostly through book learning, and had attended the occasional Sunday morning Zen Center lecture out at Green Gulch Farm. "It was San Francisco Bay Area in the eighties," he explains. "We had everybody there. I learned the basics, focused on breathing and noticing my thoughts. I'd do five minutes, ten minutes, twenty, whatever. The effect was striking. Suddenly synchronicities in my life would just start happening all the time."

Always an experimenter, a scientist at heart, Henry would experience these synchronicities and think: that's statistically impossible. He figured there must be some unknown rule behind the phenomenon. "Here I am meditating, picturing things, imagining something happening and then, BOOM! There it is," he says. "That happened a lot when I was meditating regularly."

Henry found this unusual ability quite useful while he was building his first business, an early Internet service that pioneered multimedia. He sold that company for eight figures in 1998.

"I could literally see things into existence," he recalls. "At a certain point, I started to feel like I was cheating and even started feeling a little bit guilty. I led the sale of the company for eight figures and ended up with a pile of money. Overnight, I had these stockbrokers calling with crazy offers to make five, ten times my money. Two days before, I couldn't possibly get access to that level of trading simply because I wasn't wealthy. Then, all of a sudden, I had this bank account and these guys are calling me saying, 'Buy ten thousand worth of stock at this mornings price, and you can sell it right now for 30 thousand. It's a special arrangement for our high net worth customers.' I'm sitting there, talking to him on the phone, and I just felt icky about it. I said, 'No. that's just wrong.'"

The prospect of making money by way of advantage or "special arrangement" produced a physical response of recoil. Making money purely because he already had money seemed to lack integrity. Years later, he would recognize it as yet another moment when his body steered him toward a higher purpose.

By then, Henry was a family man. With a wife and two young children, he started a second business, a too-early social network tool for an industry that hadn't yet emerged. While working to grow that business, the demands on his time and attention made it nearly impossible to set aside time to meditate.

"Weird thing happened," he says. "When I wasn't meditating, the synchronicities all but stopped."

Flow, Intuition, and Synchronicity

As a twenty-something Henry didn't know what experience has since revealed. As it turns out, meditation strengthens a person's intuition and allows us to access a state of flow. Thus, the increased synchronicities. In fact, flow seems to be a precondition for invoking synchronicities and the ideal state to tap into the vast, expansive knowing characteristic of intuition. We don't mean to suggest that this is a linear progression: meditation →intuition →flow →synchronicities. It's more circular wherein each feeds into and thus increases the other. We could even call it an upward spiral. The more you meditate, the more trust you have in your intuition, the more you can access higher and higher states of flow, the more synchronicities occur. And so it goes.

That's not to say we can make synchronicities happen, rather we can create the conditions for them to arise in a way more aligned with our purpose (provided we are paying attention to that purpose). When you have the skills to access a state of flow, you're more likely to both invoke and notice synchronicities when they show up.

Truth be told, intuitive flashes happen all the time. They often occur without our knowing until after the fact. Ever had the experience of reflecting on an unhappy circumstance and realizing you had a bad feeling about it early on? In retrospect, the message in your intuitive hit is clear: "Don't go there," or some equivalent. We get these signals all the time. If we trust our intuition, they are easy to hear and decipher. If we don't, they are easy to dismiss or ignore. At times, we miss the signal altogether. We let the rational mind assert its agenda and determine yay or nay. But intuition draws from a much larger data-set when making decisions. It understands far more than the conscious mind can grasp, and is less concerned with what's reasonable. In that sense, intuition has its finger on a different pulse altogether. Said simply: intuition is more than the sum of its parts.

On the flip side of the signals that show up as "a bad-feeling" are the good-feeling intuitive hits that often lead to surprising and delightful results. Surely, you've had such experiences. Can you call to mind an example? Can you feel the way the flush of "Yes, this is good" registered in your body? See if you can create that feeling now about an important goal or aspiration. You've just stepped onto that upward spiral. Curious, isn't it? Can you sense how your body just seems to know what's in alignment with your innermost self, your treasured dreams? This is what some have called the "upward pull of heaven's gate."

Talk with an open-minded friend and share how these intuitive knowings show up. Discuss your own experience of the "yes" or "no" signals (sometimes referred to as a "sixth sense") and ask your friend if they sometimes get this type of gut feeling. Run a little experiment and see what happens when you speak with others about your unusual experiences. We'll look at this in more detail when we discuss what author Elizabeth Lloyd Mayer has to say in her book, *Extraordinary Knowing* in Chapter Six.

A Higher Platform For Living

The best and perhaps only place to step onto the upward spiral is to start right where you are. Ask yourself: what kind of flow am I living in—positive or negative? Take stock of your mental state. It's a simple form of meditation. You simply notice your state of mind. Witness the flow of thoughts. Is your mind full of chatter? What of your emotional body? Are you in a swirl of fear and negativity? Be careful not to judge yourself. Like most people, you've been conditioned to feed your fears with worry. It's habitual: we stew on things and thereby amplify angry or upset feelings. But if you accept whatever you find, you may notice that states of fear, anger, negativity, and regret can become your friend if you allow them to show you the way back to a high flow state. The key is to avoid making your feelings wrong. Negativity can actually shut down intuition. When you find yourself in a negative state of mind, it's important to be gentle with yourself rather than compound it by being hard on yourself. Soften and open when you take stock in this way. Remember what Dan's sensei recommended? The aim is to "head into your most fearful place." This requires courage, awareness and intention. Simply looking honestly at the contents of your mind, strengthening your Witness by developing the ability to observe yourself from a relatively objective point of view, puts you on a higher platform. From this higher place, you can readily develop the ability to observe yourself from a relatively objective point of view. From there, you can move into the upward spiral and begin to explore what it's like to be in a state of flow.

In his role as Vice President of the Royal Roads University Foundation, Dan's responsibilities included fundraising. He recalls an afternoon when he was introduced to a very successful real estate magnate. During lunch with Dan and the President of the university, the man shared his grief over the loss of his only son who had committed suicide several years before.

"I could see that he was still devastated," Dan explained. "Absolutely ruined."

In the years since his son's death, the man had started seeking more meaning and purpose. Making money in the real estate market just didn't cut it anymore. He turned his life around and began concentrating on leadership. He spent his days figuring out ways to foster more authenticity and genuine leadership in business.

"It was a very unusual first meeting," Dan recalls. "Usually it takes months, even years to build a relationship with a philanthropist before you ever engage in a discussion about money."

But Dan's intuition had a finger on that different pulse. After an hour and a half lunch meeting, while walking down the stairs to leave the President's office, Dan's intuition gave him a powerful nudge.

He did not hesitate or stop to think it through; he simply followed his intuition's lead and said, "So, how would you like to create a leadership institute in your son's name to honor him?"

The man replied, "How much would that cost?" When Dan gave him a number, he said, "Okay, let's do it."

At times, all the rules, structures, and stages are irrelevant. The right moment just arrives. When Dan spoke with the man a year or so later, he acknowledged that fact by saying, "I only did it because it felt so right in that moment."

From Dan's perspective, the man knew that he'd been truly seen and heard in both his grief and his desire to serve. That seeing allowed Dan to tap into a higher order of reality. The Institute in honor of the man's son still exists to this day.

When Dan shared this story with Henry in a meeting in 2013, Henry realized that he could use a similar approach in his business. It became clear to him that he needed to transform himself in order to effect transformation in his clients. The patterns that we "see" out there are simple reflections of our inner world. Henry decided to focus on his own practice with Dan.

Chapter Four

Meditation For Busy People

Dan and Henry first met in 2003 while they were both working for Democrat Dennis Kucinich's presidential primary campaign. Many years later, in the spring of 2013, Dan Spinner was living in Victoria, Canada and became curious about using technology to broaden his coaching practice and go to scale. He wanted to work with more people than he could reach one-to-one. It wasn't clear to him what form that would take, but he'd put out a specific request to the Universe to send him deeply spiritual technology partners. He started meditating, using visualizations to imagine a specific outcome: collaborating with experts.

The idea first occurred to him while attending the Wisdom 2.0 Conference in San Francisco, then again while in a meeting with executives at the FCC and

Census Bureau. In Henry's professional opinion, the corporate and bureaucratic culture typical of government was hindering efforts to modernize technology. Attempts at improvement were outright crippled by the intransigent, hardened, blame-oriented institutions within the Federal Government.

The Henry Hypothesis: "I Have Five Minutes"

On May 9th, 2013, Henry called Dan to reboot their friendship. At the same time, several hundred miles south in Lafayette CA, Henry Poole began visualizing bringing meditation practices into, of all places, the US government. At the time, CivicActions, the company Henry co-founded in 2004, was working with the Department of Defense, the White House and other agencies. In his consulting role, Henry had become keenly aware that many of the people working in those high-pressure environments were in a constant state of stress and not able to fully utilize the powers of empathy and compassion needed to work through differences effectively. Even though his clients didn't necessarily articulate "listening to hearts of others" as a value, the cost of relying primarily on the thinking mind in the workplace was crystal clear to Henry. "People who spend much of their time in a state of fear tend to lose the ability to see others as allies. They often get tricked by their egos and fight to be right and make others wrong. This strengthens the thinking mind and tends to cripple creativity, collaboration and innovation, all of which rely on a sense of trust and deep connections with others."

When Dan asked Henry why he had called, Henry simply said, "I just felt like I should." For Dan, this supposedly random occurrence wasn't random in the least; it was a response to the intentional field he'd been generating in the weeks prior.

The two men caught each other up on significant events that had happened in each of their lives since they last spoke. The conversation then veered off into Henry's interest in transforming the world. Awhile later, they started talking about meditation. Knowing that Dan had been a meditator for many years, Henry asked him to help him develop a practice of his own. "But I'm a busy guy," he told Dan. "I'm not going to sit and do 20, 30, 40 minutes. I need to get the benefit of meditation in a short period of time." He reasoned that, if time is an illusion, why not five minutes instead of twenty?

Dan, in turn, shared his interest in increasing the impact of his work through emerging technology. At that moment, Henry and Dan decided to schedule a weekly call to brainstorm and share their thoughts on how they might combine forces and work together. They agreed there was a desperate need to develop new language and new tools for specific networks of people. In order for these ideas to gain acceptance, they would have to back up their recommendations with science. Fortunately, there was more and more research being done on meditation that evidenced its effectiveness. They were certain they could easily make the case for the new language and tools by citing scientific evidence that mediation improved connectivity, productivity and teamwork among workers. They became excited about the possibilities.

In the interest of exploring ways to transform government, Henry and his Board of Directors at CivicActions had recently enrolled in a course at Search Inside Yourself Leadership Institute (SIYLI), a Google spin-off. SIYLI had developed a very effective methodology for increasing the productivity of programmers by teaching them meditation practices. One of Henry's key takeaways from the SIYLI training was that other course participants were especially intrigued by a discussion about curiosity as it relates to productivity. This mapped onto his conversations with Dan and dovetailed beautifully with the language and tools they were developing.

During the weekly calls with Dan, Henry became clear that the struggle among federal government employees, while more aggravated, was similar to his own struggle. Like him, they were just too busy and stressed to keep up a daily meditation practice. For Henry, the logic and obvious benefits of meditation did not provide sufficient motivation to incorporate a daily practice into his busy schedule. He knew from experience the practice would pay-off handsomely, but just couldn't break his habit of booking himself for back to back meetings, adding endless to-dos to his list, and doing dad-duty for his two pre-adolescent boys about to enter their teenage years.

He asked Dan to work with him, but placed a difficult limitation on the endeavor: he wanted to do only five minute meditations. Furthermore, Henry needed a coach or a mindfulness buddy, much as people need running or lifting partners, to make them more likely to do their training. Few people will let a partner down by not showing up, or showing up with a nonchalant attitude.

Dan felt a bit challenged by Henry's odd request. More than a life coach, he'd been meditating and teaching meditation for years, always in the 20 minute or more style. He, like so many others in the mindfulness community, had always stood on the widely accepted belief that 20 minutes was a bare minimum and 40 minutes was the preferred duration for meditators if they wanted to advance toward the ultimate goal of "enlightenment."

"Five minutes, eh?" Dan said in response to Henry's caveat. "That's quite a departure from traditional practice."

Over the next several weeks, the two men mulled over the five minute requirement. Henry kept insisting that it would be impossible for him to commit to a longer block of time. Dan was skeptical at first. To his way of thinking, it was important to set aside a minimum of 20 minutes to get into the brainwave state that provided a true benefit. But he could tell that this issue would be a deal-breaker, and the more he thought about it, the more the idea of a short-but-sweet practice grew in appeal. So he set aside his doubts and agreed to give it a whirl, rising to the challenge by employing one of his firmly held convictions: that time is an illusion.

Basic Structure and The Next Evolution

Perhaps the twenty minute rule-of-thumb is a questionable guideline, Dan thought. So he started to experiment with a variety of approaches, doing spontaneous guided meditations with Henry over the phone. The first five minute meditation was "Wake Up Curious #1 - Journey into Nature," which was recorded on Sept 8, 2013 with Dan Spinner leading and Adam Hibble and Henry Poole listening. After the five minutes, Dan invited Adam and Henry to comment on their experience. In the past, having a meditation buddy had been something of a crutch for a busy executive, but it turned out that having another person to share with deepened the experience. The sharing afterward invited both a human connection and an opportunity to put words to the experience. This became an essential element of their calls along with the five minute format and meditation buddy.

Meanwhile, Dan discovered that a visualization with significant transmission was as effective as the typical "clear your mind" style of meditation. He also found that the visualizations were most effective when he didn't plan or script them in advance. As for Henry, the emphasis on visualizing confirmed his earlier conviction (as well as his uncles) that group visualizations were powerful. As the experiment continued, the two met erratically at first and then weekly. Henry found the practice rewarding so he told Dan he wanted to put it on his busy-guy calendar.

Over the next few months, a basic structure for the five-minute practice emerged. The next evolution occurred when they invited Brooks Cole, a friend of Henry's, to join the calls. Being a card-carrying member of the Geek Squad, Brooks suggested they record the calls in a more suitable format and, in time, he began to sound-engineer the calls.

For years, Henry, Brooks and Dan had each been practicing meditation. They all noticed that a regular practice of meditating brought about almost magical connections into their life. They also noticed that maintaining a calm state of centeredness brought more and better insights. They all felt a certain clarity emerge, more ease at making decisions big and small, and more accuracy and effectiveness when problem-solving. These same benefits resulted from meditative journeys, which naturally and easily fed their curiosity.

Lucid Dreaming, Lucid Awakening

Another phenomenon that Henry, Dan and Brooks had each experienced was lucid dreaming, defined in Wikipedia as a dream during which the dreamer is aware that he or she is dreaming. The term was coined by a Dutch psychiatrist named Frederik van Eeden who came up with it in his 1913 paper, "A

Study of Dreams." But the practice predates Doctor van Eeden's study. Tibetan Buddhists have been practicing what they call "dream yoga" for a very long time. Certain indigenous cultures have been known to engage in "tribal dreaming" wherein individuals meet in "the dreamtime."

For most lucid dreamers, the aim is to develop the ability to have some degree of control over the dream characters, the narrative, and the environment in which the dream occurs. Henry, in particular, had often felt a desire to bring aspects of lucid dreaming into his waking state. He was deeply curious about this idea and wanted to explore the possibility of learning to "wake up" at will when in the midst of a busy day. He reasoned that, just as he could wake up in a dream and realize he had the power to fly (or to change a grizzly bear into a teddy bear, or do whatever he wanted in the dream state), so too he could wake up in his daily life. He craved the sweet freedom of not feeling imprisoned by his attachment to the immutable nature of time and space. What if all of his responsibilities, his ideas about reality, did not necessarily preclude him from experiencing that sweet freedom?

One of the techniques used by lucid dreamers is to create a personal anchor they can then observe when it appears in a dream. The anchor then prompts the dreamer to recognize that they can actually observe what is occurring in the dreams. The anchor, in effect, puts the dreamer is a state where they can have agency and dream intentionally. In other words, they can claim their power within the dream and thus move from an unconscious to a semi-conscious state. Henry thought that perhaps the waking state could be "hacked" in a similar way. Maybe the never ending thoughts could be interrupted by noticing that he was not just his thoughts. Maybe practicing short but intense meditations could create an anchor like that used by the lucid dreamer. Could that enable him to essentially turn on his natural curiosity at any moment in daily life by simply making the choice to wake up curious?

When first attempting to remember your dreams, proponents of Lucid Dreaming recommend keeping a dream journal. The act of attempting to translate dreams into words somehow makes them both more accessible and memorable. The sharing between people in the Wacuri Method is similar — it reifies the experience of meditation.

Perhaps, anyone can wake up to their natural curiosity and see the vast potential in normal life. This became the inspiration for the method, which eventually was named Wacuri, a short form of "waking up curious."

Over the course of several years, the Wacuri Method was honed into a set of best practices and guidelines presented in Chapter Eight. The system was born from and shaped by the necessity of a personal growth system applicable to busy executives. As a student of traditional meditation practices, Dan knew this meant stepping into the unknown, but he used his pre-existing knowledge base to hone the method.

Mindfulness In Its Many Forms

What does it mean to be mindful? In the simplest sense, mindfulness is an intentional process whereby a person gets up close and personal with their own experience.

That may sound strange at first. Up close and personal? What is experience if not up close and personal? But think about it. You get out of bed in the morning and go about your day. Most of what you do is somewhat routine and requires little attention or thought. All the while, from the moment you wake up, a stream of thoughts is flowing through your mind. Sometimes that thought stream is full of plans and new ideas. More often than not, however, the stream is fairly mundane. Most of the thoughts that float through your mind are totally unoriginal. You've thought them all before in one form or another. So off you go, doing what you do just like every other day. You have tasks to complete, problems to solve, people to answer to, calls to make, errands to run, the list goes on and on. Such is life.

If you're like most people, your attitude fluctuates with circumstances. You enjoy yourself when life seems to be going your way, but enjoyment gets the short shrift when difficulties arise. Overall, you're pretty much on automatic, barely aware of the subconscious motivations behind your words and actions. It's not that you're mindless; it's just that you're not fully alive. Most people spend a good portion of each day suspended in a daydream, subtly disconnected from their body, dominated by thoughts about the past or the future, absorbed in a long list of to-do's and responsibilities.

Mindfulness changes all that. With roots in Buddhism and the yogic traditions, mindfulness can free you from the tyranny of everyday habit. Regular practice turns down the volume on the incessant mind-chatter that plays in the mind throughout the day. It does this, in part, by developing the ability to witness one's thoughts. This is a powerful transition. What was once totally subjective, the thought stream in your mind, becomes objectified. Instead of your thoughts having you (at times by the throat), you realize that you are having them. Even the smallest distance between you and your thoughts gives you more choice in terms of your affect or behavior. That little bit of objectivity leads to more psychological nuance and sophistication, which means your behavior can be more adaptive rather than counter-productive. In other words, you are more likely to have a choice as to your attitude and mood.

In the words of Thich Nat Hahn: "Mindfulness shows us what is happening in our bodies, our emotions, our minds, and in the world. Through mindfulness, we avoid harming ourselves and others."

The practice involves slowing down, paying attention to the breath and stream of thoughts. The benefits are manifold, from reducing depression and anxiety to improved athletic performance, and yet the process itself can be quite elusive. Forming the habit is the first and most challenging obstacle for most people. Once the habit is formed, it may take years of disciplined practice before deep states of calm are achieved.

What if we could wake up to the awesome possibilities in every moment without years of training? That is the aim of Wacuri journeys. They allow you to discover a new and relatively effortless way to relax and establish yourself as a witness, outside of what you typically consider yourself to be. This gives you the ability to be fully present in any moment of your life. Once the journey is complete, the transformative experience is made more real by sharing it with others. By verbalizing what you saw, felt, heard, and thought during the journey in the presence of others, you practice establishing yourself as a witness of your body and mind rather than fully identify with the body as if that is yourself. In effect, by sharing your experience, you build a bridge that allows you to travel in and out of this elevated state.

In a Wacuri Journey, when "two or more have gathered" to explore new terrain, they naturally expand their ability to access what is often called non-local consciousness, i.e.: consciousness that exists independent of any individual brain.

In this way, individual expansion is affirmed by one's co-journeyers and, in turn, expands and enhances their combined consciousness. The meditation is anchored because of this sharing. Wacuri allows you to collaborate and connect deeply with others while reflecting on your own emotional response to the journey as well as any insights or discoveries. Many of us feel this deep connection as love.

Topics explored in Wacuri journeys are very wide ranging from the Transformation of Fear to the Celebration of the Beauty of a Galaxy. They are always about seeing the oneness in everything. The topic of the journey is always chosen spontaneously, on the spot, by the individual guiding the journey. Sometimes, if the person guiding that day didn't have a topic in mind, he would ask for suggestions. These innovations emerged during the semiweekly meetings held by the founders of Wacuri. They were surprised to discover what allowing the topic of the journey to arise spontaneously made possible: an effective collaborative meditation. This spontaneity requires the Journey Guide to be fully present in the moment and let the journey emerge from the deepest parts of their Being.

Relation of Wacuri to Other Meditation Methods

Meditation practices are often placed in several categories:

Focused-Attention: Focus-based meditation asks the meditator to attend to their breath, or heartbeat, or a repeated mantra, or a visual focus. Zen meditation tends to be focus-based.

Mindfulness/Open-monitoring: The meditator passively monitors the body, thoughts, sensory input, etc. without judgement.

Compassion and Loving Kindness/Automatic Self-Transcending: The meditator promotes their own benevolence toward other people.

Guided meditations are from a long tradition specifically in the Theosophical tradition as well as the Catholic tradition of Saint Ignatius de Loyola amongst others.

Contemplation: on an object such as a mandala or specific scripture.

Healing Prayer: Attention is focused on the wholeness of the individual receiving the prayer. This approach, in contrast with an active supplication that asks for someone to be healed, requires intentional focus, which is a feature of all forms of mindfulness.

The Wacuri Method has aspects of several of these approaches. At the beginning of the meditation, the journeyer is invited to focus on their posture and breathing briefly. Thereafter, the focus shifts to the object of transmission (what you are journeying to) as the journeyer naturally focuses on the voice of the journey guide. Some meditators may employ mindfulness at this point, monitoring their thoughts and observing when their mind wanders from the content of the journey. Depending on their training and practice, they may intentionally bring their attention back to the journey.

Most of the Journeys produced by Wacuri involve gratitude and a sense of connection, which is related to Compassion and Loving Kindness. Strictly speaking, Compassion is not part of the method, however, self-transcendence, (ie.: relinquishing self-centered attention to focus on the journey) is an explicit part of the method. A good journey may well bring about a small shift in consciousness, a temporary reprieve from focusing on oneself in favor of focusing on the object of transmission. In this sense, every journey aims at self-transcendence.

The Wacuri Method of social meditation and, in particular, the debrief structure, can be used for religious meditation or group prayer. It is possible to perform a journey in the mode of spontaneous prayer. For example, a historical or scriptural scene related to religious figure might be a fitting subject for a Journey.

Examples might include:

- from Buddhism: Gautama meditation beneath the Bodhi tree,
- from Christianity: the actions depicted in the 14 Stations of the Cross,
- for other Abrahamic religions: the actions of a prophet.

In general, a journey to a natural object, such as an astral nebula or a spiderweb might be given a theistic or religious flavor if the Guide so chooses. However, the Wacuri Method insists upon the spontaneity of the Journey, so non-spontaneous religious prayer or rote repetition of a creed would not be considered a Wacuri Journey. For example, repeating the Judaic Shema or the Lord's Prayer from Christianity for five minutes, or reading scripture, would not be considered a Journey. Guides who wish to do this may still use our guidelines or platform for the debrief process of social mediation, thus utilizing that aspect of our structured method for their own purposes.

Verbalization and the Method

The primary innovation in the Wacuri Method is the placement of meditation into a social context with emphasis on immediate verbalization of the experience in the presence of others. The act of verbalizing and sharing activates language pathways in the brain, strengthening the journeyer's ability to remain centered in a variety of situations beyond the pristine setting of a church, temple, a quiet place in nature, or other tranquil environment.

Humans tend to become most off-center when in the context of other humans. If we have memories (some of which may be deeply buried) of not getting the approval we wanted from our mother, father, sisters, or brothers, these will be tied to our need for connection and safety. By quickly distinguishing our ego, noticing our physical body, our thoughts and feelings, then firing the neural networks that engage our voice, the method trains us to bring mindfulness into human interactions where it might otherwise be difficult to do so.

The Case for Social Meditation

It is well known that most people find it easier to meditate in a group. But with technology making us increasingly isolated and cut-off socially (thus amplifying existential loneliness for many) we have to make a project of finding, joining, and attending a local meditation group. That is why many online communities are thriving, for better or worse.

Meditation is difficult enough without all the attempts to "brand it" or for profit that make it evermore confusing on initial approach. What are the rules and conventions? Who are the teachers and leaders? Some methods are all about the method. Others are all about the lineage. Still others revolve around a particular teacher whose charisma is the glue that holds the community together. Countless people the world over have gotten caught up in the "tractor beam" of one guru or another—again, for better or worse.

From our point of view, the need for a structured approach, one that did not require years of discipline or allegiance to a leader to receive benefit, was amply clear. To meet that need, we set out to create a safe, online, heart-based community that can reach thousands through social meditation online. We define social meditation as the shared experience of accessing Source and Higher Self. To that end, all Wacuri Journeys are designed to invoke a moment of awe about the guide's chosen topic. It is through that shared moment of awe that a sense of community is born. It's similar to what occurs when we share a moment of awe while watching a beautiful sunset with a friend and then speak about it. It's what happens when a mother and father delight in their child's first steps. That sense of awe and wonder creates a special kind of bond between those who share the experience. It also allows us to recognize our common consciousness.

In recent years, the scientific community has become interested in the physiology of awe and curiosity. There seems little doubt that as the research advances, shared awe and shared curiosity will show mutual synchronistic patterns and resonant alignment of specific physiological biometrics and psychological mood scores. We foresee a time when empirical evidence will support our theory as to the efficacy of this form of social meditation.

In sum, the entire point of social meditation online is the ease and impact factor. Many people find it is easier to meditate with others, and we know that sharing one's experience of a journey afterward generates a sense of connection with self, one's fellow journeyers, and the larger Universe.

Thus does a conscious Wake Up Curious community come into being.

Deeper Connections, Stronger Human Bonds

Dr. Dan Siegel is arguably one of the great neuroscience geeks of our time. We say that with all due respect and affection. A clinical professor of psychiatry at UCLA School of Medicine and Executive Director of the Mindsight Institute, he pioneered the field of interpersonal neurobiology and, in fact, coined the term. In a recent talk titled "A Truly Connected Life" at the Wisdom 2.0 conference, Siegel got a bit choked up when he told a story about belonging.

While conducting clinical research in Namibia, Africa, Siegel had the opportunity to spend some time with the native tribespeople. The Namibian people are of particular interest to scientists because, according to linguistic and genetic studies, they are closely related to the original human beings. Evermore remarkable is their consistently happy disposition despite the horrible famine, drought, and disease that is characteristic of their vicinity. One night, while sitting around the campfire with the locals, Siegel was chatting with one of the tribesmen through a translator. Curious about their good-natured way of life, he asked his translator to pose a pointed question to the tribesman. The translator replied, "You want me to ask him why the villagers are so happy?"

Dr. Siegel was nearly moved to tears as he shared with his audience the tribesman's explanation: "My people are happy because they belong. They belong to each other and they belong to Earth."

The villager then asked the translator to ask Siegel a question: "In America, do you feel that you belong?"

Siegel had to think about that one. His conclusion? "We have pulled ourselves out of belonging in the most unhealthy way you can imagine."

Siegel has dedicated his career to studying how we've pulled ourselves out of belonging and, more importantly, how we can reconnect with ourselves, with each other, and with our humanness and our planet. He writes for both the professional and lay audiences and has authored several New York Times Bestsellers, including: *Mind: A Journey to the Heart of Being Human*, and *The Yes Brain*. He is the Founding Editor for the Norton Professional Series on Interpersonal Neurobiology, which contains over fifty textbooks

Insofar as we have viewed the mind as the activity of the brain (which, Siegel argues, we've been doing since Hippocrates) we have created a lack of belonging. We've become alienated from ourselves, from each other, and from our environment. It's not difficult to see the results if you look around. The average person spends the lion share of their day in a trance of disconnection. We have thousands of Facebook friends, but we're suffering from an epidemic of loneliness. Technology has made it possible to connect with each other at warp speed while the tyranny of time gets more and more oppressive. How many people do you know who feel like they're in a pressure cooker because there just aren't enough hours in a day?

Fortunately, the mechanistic paradigm that fostered our current state of disconnection is starting to change. Neuroscientists and pioneers like Siegel are forging a new view of human nature in which mind comes not just from the brain. A variety of research studies have now confirmed a hypothesis put forward by Siegel and others, which suggests that mind arises from the interweaving of the brain and body (the embodied brain), from our relationships, and energy flow. That's right, energy flow. Again, quoting Siegel: "Flow just means change... Energy flow is not some mysterious thing, maybe wonderful, but not really mysterious. It's part of physics. If physics is part of science, talking about energy is scientific, even though people get nervous about it. Energy flow is what is shared in relationships."

Belonging is a basic human need. We are social animals with an inbuilt need to connect with and rely on one another. Our biology responds to human touch, the sound of a loved one's voice, to looking into another person's eyes. Consider the fact that deep in your brain you have a translator that deciphers micro-movements in the tiny muscles around another person's eyes and mouth. And it performs this feat lightening fast, with no help whatsoever from your conscious mind to make that translation. The sense you get that you "just know" what that person is feeling is real. It's also experiential evidence that you are hardwired for social interaction. But your "connection software" may need an upgrade. That is the aim of the Wacuri Method. To practice running a new program that makes it almost effortless to connect deeply with others.

At the heart of the Wacuri Method is the recognition that deeper connections make for stronger human bonds. During a Wacuri journey, connections are forged in an intentional way within the group biofield. The connections are then enhanced and deepened through sharing moments of awe. This shared biofield interaction promotes relational intelligence, adaptability, and flexible thinking. You discover and practice ways of connecting with others that are full of vitality, authenticity and openness. The method affords you a wonderful opportunity to do exactly that after the journey by sharing your experience with your fellow travelers. We will talk in detail about the impact of this type of sharing in Chapter Six.

CHAPTER FIVE

EVOLUTION'S SECRET: THE HUNGER FOR WHAT'S NEW AND BETTER

"I have no special talents. I am only passionately curious."

~Albert Einstein

When we think about a great mind like Einstein, we tend to envision him at a blackboard covered with equations, working out $E=Mc2$. But Einstein did not arrive at his outlandish realizations while standing at the drawing board. He arrived at them while taking flights of fancy in his favorite overstuffed chair.

In one famous story, Einstein would imagine himself hovering over a train. The train would go faster and faster and faster through space. Curious to see what would happen to the atoms of the train as the speed of light was approached, he would sit back and watch. As the train approached the speed of light, he would simply observe. He conducted these thought experiments in a state of reverie, much as Nikolas Tesla did in his process of discovery.

The "Ah-Ha!" realizations he would have in this state showed him principles that had not been identified before. Then he would go to the chalkboard and work it out from there.

Einstein had a strong relationship with his wife that gave him a deep sense of belonging, thus affording him the safety to venture outside common ideas of authority.

Enter Through the Imaginal Realm

In a reversal of the learning process whereby we climb the ladder of understanding rung by rung, Einstein followed his curiosity and enlisted his imagination to arrive at a higher level. From that elevated platform he could then unfurl a rope ladder of reason, using mathematics to construct each rung. Scientific materialists could then climb up and see the natural law that had always been there, just beyond their view. The entryway to higher understanding, in this case, was the imaginal realm.

Once the rope ladder was in place, others could use Einstein's formulas to climb up to his level of understanding and test his discovery. Once empirical examination proved the veracity of his insight, that understanding became shared knowledge.

It is worth noting here that the empiricists could not have unfurled the rope ladder from the ground up.

Likewise, Tesla had tremendous precision in his imagination. He would create machines in his mind, start them running, then go off and do something else. Later, he would come back and check the machines for wear. Tesla was a true savant in the use of imagination. He came to most of his ideas by creating precise constructions in his mind. A unique feature of many of his creations was autonomy. He would actually set them free to take on a life of their own.

The key attribute of these brilliant idealists was not just their individual mind, but also their ability to share their insights in words and pictures.

This process of invention, of imagining things into existence, occurs along a continuum in everyday life.

We all live in a constructed reality along a full spectrum from pure imagination to what's really real. The takeaway from this glimpse of the imaginal realm that Einstein and Tesla inhabited is this: your mind is the gateway. With the slightest effort, you can exert your imagination and enter the realm of what's possible. Once there, you can bring a vague reality out of the fog and begin to give it definition. Some such inventions can be left to define themselves. Others need your continued effort to become defined. Once what you've imagined reaches a point of sufficient definition, it is simply there, right in front of you.

The Primal Urge to Explore

You don't have to be an Einstein to discover new terrain, and you don't need an imagination as wild as Tesla's to be moved by curiosity. The primal urge to explore is core to every human being and, apparently, most felines. Thus the cat with nine lives. Why would a cat need nine lives? Because curiosity leads it into all sorts of danger. Likewise, human beings.

We learn by exploring our environment, through trial and error, following our curiosity wherever it leads. We are guided by our senses and our inbuilt need to know about the world around us. Watch little children explore their surroundings and this becomes obvious. They put this or that in their mouths with little regard for cleanliness or consequences. They ask question after question as the big wide world clamors around them. They love picking things up and exploring weight, color, and texture long before the concept of weight, color, and texture dawn. They stick fingers wherever fingers will fit, even into places fingers aren't meant to go. Humans are born with a compelling need to explore and understand their environment. Ultimately, we may be better able to master our environment when we feel safe to explore it, then verbalize and share what we discover with others.

As the environment we inhabit expands in depth and dimension, our hunger to know carries us into ever broader and deeper territory. We're constantly on the move, exploring what's possible physically, mentally, emotionally, and spiritually. It matters not if the realms we explore are material or immaterial. Humans have an abundance of curiosity to bring to the table. Meanwhile, evolution continues its relentless advance in a discontinuous fashion, propelled by crisis and stress. Throughout time, curiosity has led the way to untold breakthroughs and revolutions in response to the pressure-cooker of existence. Paired with our inbuilt survival mandate, the hunger to know is a powerful evolutionary driver. In that sense, curiosity is evolution's handmaiden, the sine qua non of expansion and innovation.

Sadly, as we grow older in a materialistic world such as ours, we often begin to feel less safe to share our experiences. Our youthful curiosity often leads us to believe that we actually know things to be true that, in fact, may or may not be. Sometimes we are so convinced we're right, we become over-identified with what we think we know. When the ego takes over our sense of who we are, it slows down the constant questioning of the child's mind and, in so doing, narrows the scope of our curiosity. Our loved ones tell us, "Do not talk to trees!" The culture at large leads us to believe that our consciousness is local. If we don't go along with these social norms, our all-important feeling of belonging may start to erode. This is how we are trained to see ourselves as separate and disconnected. In extreme cases we can become automatons. Our ability to verbalize experiences of awe and wonder are constantly under threat while, at the same time, our thirst for belonging and the need to "fit in" increases. This is how we become alienated from our true selves.

Social Curiosity, Social Media, and Social Intelligence

This primal urge is an individual imperative that encompasses our social environment as well. In the world as we know it in the early 21st century, a large segment of the population inhabits a social environment that includes a virtual life online. All we have to do is reach for a smartphone for instant access to friends near and far. And while Facebook, Twitter, Instagram, SnapChat and other platforms of their ilk look and feel as if they are brand new territory (at least to those of us over 25), they also recapitulate an ancient need. We understand ourselves (and our place in the cosmic order) within the context of our social sphere. Science calls it social curiosity.

Said simply: we're innately curious about our fellow humans. The driver behind this curiosity is the desire to belong. Otherness intrigues us. We want and need to know what those we associate with are made of, and we have untold ways of sussing each other out. This becomes evermore intriguing and complex when we can connect with people around the globe with just a few keystrokes. Geographic and cultural differences make faraway friends and acquaintances all the more curious, adding to the intrigue, and offering us a new opportunity to find that sense of belonging we all crave.

Social media, like most innovations, brings with it a new set of problems. We're more connected than ever and yet, at the same time, beleaguered by the loneliness and isolation that cyber contact engenders. Left unchecked and unaddressed, such feelings readily turn into depression. A whole swath of humanity is awash with negative emotions that result directly from their involvement in social media. Whenever a new problem like this reaches a fever pitch, that very crisis often compels further evolution.

In this case, it is the nature and quality of our social intelligence that wants to evolve. How much time are we willing to spend embroiled in the virtual version of a cafeteria food fight on Twitter? Plenty, it seems, until and unless we discover an alternative that satisfies the greater part of who and what we are as social beings.

This begs the question: are we or aren't we a better social animal than social media has revealed us to be? We are, after all, the same species that have gathered together in a sacred way over millennia. Baptists and Calvinists call this coming together communion.

What to do in the face of social stressors and the crazy machine that amplifies our lesser angels and those nefarious behaviors that undermine rather than amplify the eternal verities of beauty, goodness, and truth? How do we coax our lower nature to allow our higher nature to rule the day?

It's a compelling moment, evolutionarily speaking, where we have a window of opportunity to come together and bring what Abraham Lincoln termed our "better angels" to the table.

A Benevolent Platform to Call Out Our Higher Nature

We foresee virtual sacred spaces to function alongside the social media giants—benevolent platforms for coming together with a clear intent to call out our higher nature. We see it as a scaling cyber-sangha, a word in Buddhism that means "beloved community" or a group of friends practicing the dharma together in order to bring about and to maintain awareness.

When the Twitter food fight gets too messy, we all need an escape route. We envision places of sanctuary that are as easy to access as opening an app on your smartphone. That's what we've set out to do.

We are not unique in our desire to escape the nastiness that has become socially acceptable online. There are any number of attempts to find islands of sanity. The catchwords of the day, from mindfulness to sustainability, reflect the zeitgeist. The general trend toward greater awareness has reached a point of no return. We all feel the need for a pressure-relief valve. Provisions for that are already up and running as the popularity of apps such as Headspace®, Calm, and Insight Timer attest.

With each of those innovative platforms, however, users are still doing the work of meditating and becoming more mindful alone. The current apps afford users a meditative experience — a virtual zafu (meditation pillow) of sorts — but they fall short when it comes to increasing connection. Thus the need for social meditation and, more specifically, social meditation apps.

Before we explore this further, let's take a look at what science has to say about our curious nature.

The 5-Type Model of Curiosity

Research psychologists study curiosity in order to better understand its starring role in human cognition, learning, and motivation. Over the years, researchers have advanced numerous theories as to the practical utility of curiosity. What they typically realize along the way is that curiosity has a surprising impact on our emotional lives. Of particular interest to the Wake Up Curious approach is the pairing of our curious nature with the reward circuitry in the human brain.

We all know the feeling — that rewarding sense of satisfaction when we resolve an ambiguous situation. Surely you've experienced the feeling of relief that comes with vanquishing your uncertainty about some unknown. Think back on the last time you managed to figure your way out of some vexing happenstance. Once you managed to overcome the challenge, you felt uplifted, yes? The reward center in your brain is responsible for that payoff.

The rewards of curiosity, that subtle state-change we experience as relief or satisfaction, comes in subtler ways as well. It's why we love a good novel. The plot lines converge, the story comes full circle and, alas, we can relax in our newly found understanding of what makes the characters tick. And we all know that lovely tension relief that comes when you finally know who won, whodunit, or who got the girl.

From a psychological perspective, curiosity is also an essential part of cognition, how we think about and relate to the world of ideas. We can easily see how the people, places, and things we get curious about reach their tendrils into our emotions and memories. Likewise our compelling urge to feed our curiosity with novel experience weaves its way into our daydreams and thoughts of the future. It doesn't take a Ph.D. to know that the feeling of being curious, the arousal that comes with even the subtlest intrigue, is a pleasure all its own. Pleasure seeking creatures that we are, we're psychologically predisposed to follow our curiosity, regardless of whether it gets satisfied or not.

In a series of studies conducted at George Mason University and led by Todd Kashdan, competing theories coalesced when researchers reviewed data collected from a variety of research projects involving nearly 4,000 adults. What emerged for Kashdan and his team was a new model for curiosity. In this new model, they identified five distinct faces of this oh-so-very human quality of consciousness.

Let's take a moment to see if those faces (or "factors" as the researchers call them) ring true in your experience. Set aside a few minutes and ask yourself these questions:

1. When was the last time I felt joyful while exploring something new? What was that

something? How did the discovery process feel?

2. Have I ever felt a subtle (or not-so subtle) arousal when I needed more knowledge or understanding before I could settle on my next move? Was there mental, physical, or emotional tension associated with not having enough information to know who's who or what's what?

3. Do I find myself interested in other people? Am I a person who listens to gossip or enjoys gossiping about other people? How often do I concern myself with what another person might do or say?

4. How well do I manage the stressful situations that pop up on a regular basis? Am I adaptable or do I tend to hang out in my comfort zone? Can I readily shift gears and come up with a Plan B when Plan A is thwarted by an unexpected turn of events?

5. Am I prone to thrill seeking, attracted to the unusual, drawn in by the promise of more and better? Do I go for it when there's a risk involved or proceed with caution, ever alert to avoid potential dangers?

You have just begun to explore what Kashdan named "The Five-Dimensional Curiosity Scale" or, more simply, 5DC. The specific five dimensions identified by Kasdan's research team are: Joyous Exploration, Deprivation Sensitivity, Social Curiosity, Stress Tolerance, and Thrill Seeking.

Let's take a moment and double down on each of these. We encourage you to reflect on your own experience through this 5D lens.

1. Joyous Exploration. This face of curiosity finds you in awe of whatever it is you have stumbled upon. It might be a magical garden or meadow, the allure of a new lover, or exotic destination. It might be the low-level thrill that keeps you turning the pages of a novel or the giggling, irresistible anticipation of what will happen in the next episode of your latest Netflix fixation.

2. "Gotta Know" curiosity (aka, Deprivation Sensitivity). This is that often uneasy feeling you get when you're at a disadvantage due to lack of knowledge. The knowledge gap can be a simple one such as "What's that dripping sound?" Or it can be as complex as "What will it take to patent my brilliant invention and get a startup funded?" Curiosity steps in to close the gap in your knowledge base and fill in your understanding of the current situation. You

instinctively know that your "need to know" is mission-critical. Without that added know-how or detailed information, you can't take effective action.

3. Social Curiosity. This is the flavor of curiosity that finds you hungry for information about another person or group. It's what gets you angling for a chance to watch, engage or otherwise rub elbows with others of your own kind. Social curiosity is responsible for helping us locate and, if we're fortunate, bond with those of like heart and mind.

4. Stress Tolerance. At first glance, it's not obvious what the admonition "Deal With It!" has to do with curiosity. But consider what this colloquialism points to and you'll bump into our inbuilt sense that we must tolerate, and even embrace, the discomfort that goes hand-in-hand with a new experience. You need this dimension of curiosity to navigate beyond the boundaries of your comfort zone, whether that journey finds you learning to kite-board or starting a new job.

5. Thrill Seeking. Some people live for the thrill of taking the big risks, but even if you wouldn't dream of BASE jumping, you do get juiced up when you approach the new and exciting. You get butterflies in your stomach

before stepping on stage, sweat bullets on a first date, feel terrified when you go up 3,000 feet for your first tandem jump from an airplane. In each case, you do much more than tolerate that anxiety; you overcome it and get a thrilling jolt of energy that takes you far beyond the ordinary day-to-day of your life.

Curiously, researchers found a high correlation between these various faces of curiosity and measures of well-being. Moreover, using this model, Kashdan and his colleagues identified four types of curious people. Most of us (well, 56% of subjects studied anyway) fall equally into the categories of what researchers call "The Fascinated" or the "Problem Solvers." Another 25% of the subjects studied were "Empathizers" and 19% were "Avoiders." What set these groups apart were differences in passionate interests, areas of expertise, consumer behavior, and use of social media.

Perhaps the most notable insight to arise from this research is that we humans are not nearly as one-dimensional as we once thought when it comes to our curious nature. Prior to this model, it was assumed that curiosity existed on a one-dimensional continuum with the incurious dolts on one end and the highly curious (and readily piqued) explorers, thrill-seekers, and inventors on the other. Not so, according to Kashdan and his colleagues.

With a deeper, wider, multi-dimensional understanding of the nature of curiosity, we gain a deeper and wider perspective on how this vital quality can be harnessed to our benefit and put to use in service of a fulfilling existence.

Kashdan is far from the first to identify different types of curiosity. In 1860, William James, widely regarded as the father of American psychology, made the distinction between common curiosity and scientific curiosity. It's worth noting that he drew this distinction around the same time that he and Charles Sanders Peirce were establishing the philosophical tradition of pragmatism.

James considered the common form of curiosity a mere "biological function," a human instinct that gets activated in the presence of something new. In contrast, the scientific expression of curiosity was a higher order altogether, akin to "metaphysical wonder." On the one hand, we have our everyday, common curiosity derived from "the practical instinctive root" that is hard-wired to our basic desire nature. On the other hand, James pointed out, we have scientific curiosity, which is piqued when "the philosophical brain... responds to an inconsistency or a gap in its knowledge." Sounds a bit like Kashdan's deprivation sensitivity, yes?

Nearly 100 years later, in the mid 20th century, curiosity came to the fore of psychological research, primarily due to the work of Daniel Berlyne. Educated at Cambridge, Berlyne went on to do his Ph.D. on... you guessed it... curiosity. In so doing, he pioneered the enormous body of research we now have on the subject.

These days, we have British journalist Ian Leslie to thank for his delightful book, *Curious: The Desire to Know and Why Your Future Depends On It* (Perseus Books, 2014). In it, Leslie reviews the science on the topic and offers a practical approach for harnessing it for the greater good. We agree with Leslie on innumerable points and especially appreciate the frame he creates by naming curiosity "a life force."

A Trait Not Just A State

Let's look at the physiology of curiosity for a moment. We have an enormous amount of scientific data on the physiology of stress. We also have an increasing amount of science on the physiology of calm, which is the opposite of stress. Now we're beginning to understand the neurophysiology of curiosity.

A specific part of the brain, the inera, lights up when we're alert and curious. When something captures our attention and we're trying to understand, this part of the brain becomes active. In this sense, curiosity is literally a state of mind. In the science community, that's how our curious nature is viewed—as a state rather than a trait. One of the many aims of the Wacuri Method is to "train and entrain" our curiosity. The aim is to activate latent potentials of the holographic organism of consciousness that we are. But before we get too far out there, let's double down and look at this distinction of state versus a trait.

When we talk about a state, we're referring to a mental and emotional condition that is specific to time and place. For most people, states tend to fluctuate with external circumstances. For example, let's say you go to your daughter's dance performance. On the way there, you are in a state of anticipation. You're excited to see her perform for the first time on stage. She's been talking about the recital for weeks and practicing in her room after school. You know how much this means to her. Your mental and emotional state is one of care and concern, mixed with a heavy dose of motherly or fatherly love. When it's time for your child to do her solo, your state becomes ever more amplified. You're on the edge of your seat, hyper-aware of her every move, streaming your love toward her from the third row. When it's over, your state changes again. Now you're thrilled she did so well. As the evening goes on, you relax into a state of deep satisfaction and parental pride.

Let's take another example, one that doesn't involve other people. Let's say you're on vacation somewhere near the ocean. You wake up early one morning and decide to take a walk. You deliberately break from your usual routine of making a cup of coffee upon waking, put on your flip-flops, and head out the door. You hit the sand just as the horizon starts blazing with the dawn. You decide to sit on the dunes and watch the sunrise. It's incredible. You enter a state of deep gratitude and awe that lingers throughout the morning.

Whatever your state—be it joy, confusion, upset, exhilaration, or excitement—it will, in time, fade and give way to another state. Over the course of a day or week, we tend to go in and out of various states as the content of our mental and emotional body shifts. States don't necessarily stay, or build on themselves. They're periodic.

Traits, on the other hand, are lasting features of personality. They build on themselves and combine in specific ways that make your perspective and your behavioral tendencies totally unique to you. Traits, unlike states, sustain over time and don't tend to change without considerable (even unnatural) effort. People who tend to be sloppy don't just outgrow it and turn into neatniks. A man or woman who keeps a Zen environment will find it difficult to relax if all is not in order. Such a person would be hard pressed to live "happily ever after" while sharing home and hearth with a spouse who is perfectly comfortable when surrounded by chaos. You likely know people on both ends of the spectrum. There are those who always clear their desk and put their pens away at the end of the day. And there are those whose desk is piled high with papers in what appears to be complete disarray, and yet they know exactly where everything is among the madness.

It is our contention that curiosity can be both state-specific and cultivated as a trait. Our intention with the Wacuri Method is exactly that: to cultivate curiosity. We do that with curated guided journeys. We don't imagine and won't go so far as to suggest that people will do one journey and suddenly transform. However, early testing suggests that the more often an individual takes a Wacuri Journey and participates in the sharing afterward, the more the method impacts who they are. In eight weeks time (the time frame suggested by our Scientific Advisory Council), doing two or three journeys each week, participants who found themselves in a state of flow while on a journey had greater access to flow in daily life. In other words, the state of curiosity had the potential to become a trait. If this latent potential is actualized might the incurious person become a curious person? And what if that person's very psychology could become more complex and sophisticated in the process? Curious, yes? What might happen when you do Wacuri Journeys on a regular basis over time? It's exciting to think about how you might feel in the future if curiosity became a stable feature of your personality, not merely a state, but a trait.

Your Curiosity Has Been Hijacked

Like most people, you're a naturally curious person. Your curious nature takes various forms and serves different ends. We've seen that some expressions of curiosity add value to your life while others add little, and still others actually rob you of precious vital energy when this wonderful, evolutionary impulse gets hijacked by the machine.

We live in a world where temptations abound, where every search you type into your browser is tracked, fed into an algorithm, and used to serve up evermore customized temptations. At every turn, you are induced and seduced to buy, buy, buy. Say you start thinking it would be nice to have a Ginsu knife. Or perhaps you're curious how much a Ginsu knife would cost because you'd like to buy one for your kitchen-obsessed relative as a birthday gift. You search Ginsu knife on Google and browse the results. Later that afternoon, you go to thesaurus.com, innocently looking for synonyms for the word temptation. In the banner at the top of the page are photos of not one, not two, but seven Ginsu knives for you to choose from. In the service of commerce, your curiosity has been hijacked. And the cyberspace sales force will continue to sell you Ginsu knives long after you lose interest or make a purchase.

Likewise, AI, social media, network TV and YouTube will hijack your curiosity in service of political, business or other agendas. Whether it's election fraud or climate change, Buddhist teachings or raw food recipes, your curious nature can lead you down all sorts of rabbit holes. Unlike genuine curiosity that leads to a satisfying payoff, induced curiosity is synthetic. You think you'll feel satisfied, go further down the rabbit hole, but come up empty every time. You think you're going to learn something, but it's just the algorithm doing a sleight-of-hand to sell you a bill of goods. Click-bait serves up a link to "Discover Jamaica" but it turns out to be a lure to get you to buy into a timeshare. Maybe you open a browser to help your son with his chemistry homework; the results offer what looks to be a promising chemistry refresher course so you click on the link, only to discover they're really just trying to get you to donate to a scholarship fund for underprivileged kids who are interested in science. The emptiness then feeds on itself, leaving you wanting more and more. You go from Ginsu knives to a Vegematic. By then your initial curiosity has morphed into a deep hunger that generalizes to other areas of your life. You feel disconnected, in need of human connection and companionship, and suddenly find yourself wasting several hours on a dating site.

At an even subtler level, this massive drive to explore can get tangled up in a social feedback loop—gated, curtailed, or amplified by social sanction. This feedback loop tells you what you can or can't be interested in, what your tribe says is okay and not okay, where there are forbidden zones you dare not enter. Socialization and peer pressure comes in and disables your once-sovereign arm of self-empowerment. Your freedom to explore is curtailed. Most pernicious is the pressure that tells you what you can think and explore, what you can talk about and what you can't, lest you be ostracized. Rather than liberate and empower people to be curious about whatever interests them, the social sphere can act like a gag order that forbids open exploration. We've seen this throughout history with oppressive regimes that put the kibosh on our curious nature, and with religious institutions that have condemned entire swaths of humanity, labeling them "heretics" simply because their curiosity took them into unknown or forbidden territory.

How do we reclaim our innate curiosity, recognize the bait and switch dead-end for what it is, maintain our sovereignty when external forces would take away our freedom to think? The Wacuri Method offers an alternative, one that feeds your curiosity and offers soul-nourishment in the form of a deeper connection with both your fellow human beings and the world around you.

Technology has the potential to contribute to the growth of human consciousness rather than distracting us and destroying it. The Wacuri Method is designed to use straight-forward technology to allow us to experience our genuine, natural curious state.

CHAPTER SIX

GATEWAY TO THE INFINITE

Your energy body or biofield is the gateway to the infinite, and the basis of the energy body is coded in our DNA and the rhythms of our hearts. Whether you call it the light body, the biofield, chi field, aura, or subtle awareness, when you begin to explore this subtle aspect of who and what we are intentionally, it becomes self-verifying. Evidence-based energy medicine is gaining ground as the seemingly miraculous abilities that healers, Reiki masters, and energy workers possess are now becoming available to ordinary people. You can learn to utilize your own, inbuilt healing power just by deciding to avail yourself of it. Along the way, you'll get glimpses, insights, flavors, tastes, and textures of what's possible. If you pay attention, you may sense this power or feel it rushing through you.

Regardless of the degree to which you actively engage with the subtle dimensions, just by reading this book and reflecting upon these ideas, you will become more aware of it on the periphery of your consciousness.

The Biofield: A New, Yet Ancient Concept

We each have our individual energy field, and those energy fields interact substantially. Moreover, we all share a common energy field. In recent years, scientists have started calling it the biofield, although this is far from a new concept. The notion that humans can register a felt sense of the energy field around them is thousands of years old. The ancients were intimate with it, and humans have utilized this energy field actively and purposefully for millennia. Now that science is catching up, discussions of the biofield and energy medicine are becoming quite common, even in the arena of what we call "conventional medicine" as we will see later in this chapter when we talk about extraordinary knowing. As these ideas gain popularity, they will enter the mainstream much like mindfulness has in the new millennium.

In recent years, a number of scientific studies have been able to measure what ancients have been talking about for centuries. They have been able to demonstrate empirically that energy fields—electromagnetic fields, biophotons, even the sounds made by our bodies—are real and all around us. What's more, recent studies suggest that our biofields actually interact with one another through resonant exchange. This is why a person in a foul mood can impact a whole room. You've probably experienced someone whose negativity seems to "suck the oxygen out of the air." Similarly, someone who walks through the door with their face full of joy can light up a room. We sometimes say their positivity is "infectious."

How is it we can feel another person's mood? Do we really impact each other with our vibrational tone or resonance? Consider the way benevolence begets more benevolence. It's the same when we meditate. It's also the secret behind healing prayer. People don't have to be geographically close to the person or persons praying; their resonant fields can be felt remotely, and even when connecting online. That's the beauty of going on a Wacuri Journey and sharing afterward. You go on a journey, experience a shared sense of awe, and start feeling a special connection. We all know it's easier to meditate with others but no one is really sure why.

After a Wacuri meditation, we invite participants to share their experience, which results in a biofield exchange we don't yet fully understand. Nonetheless, the benefits are easy to verify experientially. Whether you access a high flow state or even a little bit of a flow state, the very act of sharing is evocative of flow. It is our theory that the interactive biofield is a stabilizing factor that impacts the energy field of each individual in the sharing group and enables them to achieve higher flow.

Of Dogs, Cats and Trees

We invite you to feel the energy of this subject matter the way you might feel a tree. If feeling a tree it too elusive with you, start with feeling a dog or cat. Not only do you share a curious nature with cats, you share a similar limbic structure in your brain and a substantial percentage of your DNA. The key is to simply have fun with it. Go on a journey. Explore the vast galaxy inside you or in space. Go be with your inner child. Explore the consciousness inside your cells. These are energetic realities with as much, if not more, substance as the chair you sit in or the phone call you made earlier today.

We also encourage you to talk about your experience in the afterglow of your energy body excursions by sharing with others. Conversation is an integrative act for the personality. It's all about teaching ourselves that we don't end at our skin. That, friends, is a glorious discovery.

In time, you'll find yourself walking around, vibing on the energy field of everything. That's right. EVERYTHING. Even the most mundane. Whether you're sitting in the gorgeous passive solar house you built yourself, or sitting on the tailgate of the station wagon you call home, contemplate the energy fields around you. Tap into the feel of just about anything or anybody and you'll realize you can play with life on a scale that can take you into your very cellular structure and beyond. You can go subatomic or go astronomic and sense the energy of that structure.

You might start by looking over at a concrete wall and saying, "Well, that's a concrete wall." Then you can zoom out and say, "No, actually, the mineral kingdom is right here." Then you can dive into the gravel, the making of concrete, the origins of the mineral kingdom. Suddenly you realize, "By God, I'm surrounded by the mineral kingdom, the very foundation of the Earth itself." All from taking a journey into a concrete wall.

So experiment. Be inventive. Let your curiosity have its way with you. Share the joy. Let life get just a little more spacious and spontaneous. Address the energy, the physics, and the spirit of whatever you encounter—it could be a slug or the night sky. Go down in, or ascend into the future. Say, "Guide me." You can access anything in your environment (or your imagination for that matter) and share the essence of it with others.

Take A Moment...

When we "take" people on a Journey, we are really inviting them to step into their multi-dimensionality. Sometimes referred to as the Higher Self or the Soul, this multidimensional you is consciousness itself. Consciousness exists beyond time and space in a constant state of flow. The normative self—what we experience as our personality—is only vaguely aware of the vastness that is its true nature. When, on occasion, we stumble into this place of pure being and encounter its deeper knowing, the contrast can be simultaneously awe-inspiring and daunting.

Revelatory in nature, the feeling/recognition that one is far more than previously imagined raises many questions. Those questions tend to shake the very ground we walk on. That can be both exhilarating and frightening at the same time. Over time, the more we embrace the notion of non-local consciousness, the more the intelligence that resides outside our own brain becomes real.

Living the illusion of separateness is painful. And yet it feels familiar and, in that sense, non-threatening. For many of us, this subtle, yet pervasive sense of being disconnected from ourselves, from one another and the Universe, is all we've ever known. Based on false assumptions about our very nature and the nature of reality itself, it makes life quite painful and difficult — but we've adapted to that pain so we barely even notice. We're numb. We put our heads down and get on with it. Business as usual.

When we ask you to "take a moment" at the start of a journey, we are inviting you to get curious, pick your head up and look around. You consider, "Hmmm… what if there's more to it than the same-old, same-old? What if there's more going on than meets the eye?" This simple act of lifting your head up activates curiosity, our natural state of aliveness, wherein we are open to discovery. It's a simple flip of the switch from a narrow perspective to a broader inquiry. We then allow our senses to encounter the Universe in all its beauty.

The Wacuri Method is a doorway into a state of being where one's True Nature can be better felt or experienced. It is meant to evoke a higher energy level, one that allows you to understand problems as opportunities and see a broader perspective. That higher perspective is full of new insights that lend clarity to choose the best direction. We can then move more effectively and joyfully toward healing, insights and creative problem-solving.

The Boundary of Self and Other

A truly satisfying conversation, to our way of thinking, is an interaction that occurs soul to soul. In that context, whatever we say comes out of that connection. You start with the question, "What is conversation?" Then zoom out a little further and ask, "What is communication?"

Initially, any given interaction with another may appear conversational. But a good observer can see that what's being said actually follows on what has already transpired energetically. As Dan Spinner is fond of saying, "The words are but an echo of energy already exchanged." In actuality, we're all interconnected energetically. That said, if we are aligned and authentic, the conversation represents the tip of the iceberg. Next time you are in a deep conversation pay attention and try to see what is actually going on beneath the surface. You may feel a current, a connection between you. We are suggesting that this is, in fact, an energetic connection—a meeting of biofields. Think about an argument or a moment of love. Can you sense the connection there?

This book is an attempt to do exactly that with you, the reader. We are connecting with you through this book. It's a transmission. You can feel it. You're connected with us. You likely have some of these very same skills. You may call them by different names, but the conversation weaves a pattern that represents and strengthens that connection. It's not about the words on the page. Words don't teach. It's about the energy connection and the words follow on that. In fact, the words reflect the energy connection.

The nature of transmission is a change in frequency; it doesn't occur in time and space. That's why the Wacuri five-minute journey method you will learn in Chapter 9 is so powerful.

We drop out of ordinary reality, however seemingly briefly, and into fuller dimensions of ourselves.

Most of all, follow what interests you and what calls your deep attention. That will allow you to journey into the essence of who you really are. From there you can make an honest and deep connection with anybody. And with anything and everything around you.

Individuality and Oneness

You might ask: "But what exactly is an energy field? How do I contact this biofield?" The best way to begin your exploration of energy fields is to adopt the position of an advocate. Said simply: you start by assuming—as a hypothesis—that energy fields exist. You stay out of the debate about it. You become a curious witness. You recognize that, yes, science has begun to corroborate the existence of biological electromagnetic fields and even more subtle energies. But who knows how long it will take for the existence of the biofield to become common knowledge? Pioneers don't wait for everyone to be on board. They go out and explore. They don't need to know what's out there; they trust their curious nature and have the courage to follow different layers of intrigue. They are happy, even delighted, to step into the unknown.

Soon you will discover that the further you go into those layers, the less your ego and the personalities of others are involved. The further out you go, the more you will connect with universal energy. The more you expand your awareness, the more the collective energy of humanity will become evident, the more the energy field of our planet and even your own cells will become real to you. There are many different layers and many different discoveries in store for you at all those levels and others as yet unimagined.

Crazy Insanity... or Sheer brilliance?

Many of us struggle with an odd paradox: we want to be truly seen by others and yet we're afraid to reveal who we really are. Henry Poole believes this peculiar behavior is a function of a fearful ego, a psychology that craves recognition and, at the same time, is terrified of rejection. Will people recognize and embrace our brilliance or will they think we're self-important or just plain crazy? Will our self-disclosure cause someone we care about to back away? Most of us decide not to run the risk. There's just too much to lose: the esteem and love of colleagues, family members, and associates. We don't want to put our hard-earned reputation or our heart on the line. So we decide to play it safe. We hold back, keep our cards close to the chest and, in the process, withhold what might just be our greatest contribution to the world and, in effect, put a cap on contentment.

Henry tells the story of what happened some years ago at a client meeting. Brooks Cole and Cody Harrington were in attendance, as well as Regis McKenna, the person who designed the Apple logo and was a coach to Steve Jobs. Midway through the meeting, Regis shared about a conversation he had with a 4-Star General who had NATO clearance. "If memory serves, this General had been nominated by President Reagan to head the Department of Defense," Henry says.

This man spoke of a group of people in Tennessee who had been doing some curious experiments. They had discovered an unconventional method of space travel by imagining a pathway through the stars. They would stand in a circle and meditate, imagine some sort of energy beacon or navigator through the stars, and an alien visitation would occur. Hearing this story, Regis' initial thought was, "Well, that's insane."

Reflecting on this seemingly outlandish tale, Henry says, "The way I looked at it, they managed to open up their perception of time and space. From that open place, they could see alternative realities and experience connections far beyond our usual sense of what time and space actually are. They stumbled into a non-ordinary reality that was nonetheless very real. But at the time, I didn't share my thoughts with Regis, lest I be rejected and lose my client."

Sounds like the stuff of science fiction, yes? Who would believe such a thing possible? Is it any wonder extraordinary discoveries such as these never make it into the headlines? Why would someone risk their reputation by sharing an experience most would consider insane?

The fear that we could be viewed as a nutcase is one many people share. We need to belong, so we avoid going too far "out of the box" of consensus reality. Henry puts it this way: "Ultimately, we're scared of being God together, and terrified of the responsibility that implies. If we were to embrace our innate divinity, we would have to admit that all of our experience and knowledge—our understanding about how to survive, about what keeps us alive—is on shaky ground. It's on shaky ground because what separates us is also what keeps us alive."

How's that for a Zen koan?

Let's double down and examine how and why we bury one of our deepest fears. Consider the ego. Consider the way it creates you, is the source of your sense of self and being in the world. At the same time, the ego has the power to kill you. As long as you see yourself as separate, as long as you remain invested in the illusion of separateness, you are stuck in a time/space pattern that is limited to what can be conceived of by the ego or the mind. This is not to vilify the ego, simply to recognize it as what it is—an instrument. In this sense, the ego is the aspect of self that generates the idea that "I am an independent being." Paradoxically, that idea is what makes it possible to be here and be with others.

In order to be with others, we have to see ourselves as separate. Exposing the connection between our body, our mind, God, and the universe—exposing the oneness of everything—would reveal that our definition of self is totally wrong. We aren't what we believe we are. If this is true, we would lose confidence in our understanding of how to survive. In essence, we would see that our entire paradigm is insane. What if our worldview is based on a fundamental misunderstanding? This is so scary that we hold desperately onto the stories that separate us from the ultimate truth that we are Source.

Our "faulty" reality-making processes

When Henry was about nine years old, his father brought home a small reel-to-reel tape recorder. While playing with his father's new electronic toy, Henry discovered something that shook his perception of reality. He'd made a recording of himself talking with his mom and was bewildered when he listened to the tape. His voice sounded like someone he did not know. His mother's voice was no different on the recording, but his own voice didn't sound at all like it did to his own ear. For Henry, this was one of those "thunderclap moments." He began to question his subjective experience of sound and, by extension, everything he knew through his senses. His curiosity quickly generalized as he realized that his experience of reality was not always the same as the reality experienced by others.

Unlike Dan, whose father inadvertently taught him not to trust authority, Henry was inducted into a worldview in which questioning authority was de rigueur. His parents not only told him as much, they demonstrated in their behavior that authority figures could not be trusted to tell you the whole story. "With a mother who taught the history of the Renaissance, the discovery of new forms of science was the norm in my mind. Stories like those of

Galileo and Da Vinci were typical dinner conversation. Experiments with ESP were common in our household. Even as a child, it was clear to me that there's more to all this than meets the eye — or any of our senses for that matter. As a boy, I reasoned that if humans can't hear radio and television broadcasts and yet they exist, it follows that humans simply don't have the right organ — or, in this case, hearing range — to register that particular signal. I've always been curious to know what other signals humans can't perceive that we have yet to discover. In our family, it was considered obvious that human discoveries were still emerging."

Henry's curiosity about the differences between his interpretation of reality and someone else's interpretation of the same event was heightened by a formative experience that occurred when he was 13. (Before we dive into the story, it's worth noting that adolescence is a time when our sense of self shifts from having a primary locus in our immediate family to being primarily located in our circle of friends.) Henry recalls how confused he felt when his best friend, Scott, mysteriously stopped returning his phone calls. In the days before texting, people actually spoke to one another on the phone and, for teenagers, these phone calls could go on for an hour or more. Henry enjoyed phone conversations with his friend, and couldn't understand why he wouldn't call him back. After a few days of silence, Scott finally accepted Henry's call. When Henry asked his friend why he hadn't answered any of the calls he'd made over the past several days, Scott said, "The way you spoke to me hurt my feelings." Another thunderclap moment. Henry had no idea that the way he'd spoken to his friend was hurtful.

This misunderstanding with his friend brought about a profound realization for Henry: he could be entirely blind when it came to seeing another person's perspective on a shared experience that "appeared" in his mind to be the same experience. He asked Scott to let him know if he did something that was hurtful in the future. In the aftermath of this relatively minor tiff with his friend, Henry became fascinated with trying to understand various people's points of view on a shared experience or interpersonal exchange. He was especially curious when the other person's perception of what had occurred contradicted his own. The more he looked into this peculiar blindness, the more Henry realized that we basically never experience an event in the same way someone else does. Said simply: sameness does not exist when it comes to shared experiences.

Alternative Realities: Embracing the Non-Ordinary

What if we exist, not in a physical universe governed by the laws of physics, but in a biocentric universe wherein everything we think of as "out there" is really just a product of our animal senses? This is the topic explored by Robert Lanza in his groundbreaking book, *Biocentrism: How Life and Consciousness are the Keys to Understanding the True Nature of the Universe*. Lanza's idea is as radical to us as the notion that "the world is round not flat" was to people in the Middle Ages. A leader in the field of applied stem cell biology, Lanza proposes that life creates the universe rather than the other way around. Building on ideas from quantum physics, biocentrism puts biology before all other scientific sciences in order to develop its theory of everything. According to Lanza, what we think of as space and time are really just forms, agreed-upon concepts, generated by sense perception; they are not external physical realities. This simple, revolutionary idea offers a whole new avenue to explore some of the most puzzling scientific conundrums of our day. It offers an entirely different way of looking at the natural laws that govern the universe and that shape us, its inhabitants.

Let's do a thought experiment here. Suppose "reality" truly is a product of our senses rather than the product of the laws of physics. Einstein is often quoted as having said: "Reality is merely an illusion, albeit a very persistent one." That persistence is largely maintained by our collective agreement on what's so. In other words, we're all generating "out there" together. It's the consensus reality that highways will continue to exist tomorrow, but do highways as such actually exist?

Now consider this. When we dream, we essentially go solo. (The exception being those who've learned to enter the dreamtime as a group, sometimes called "tribal dreaming," or those whose have telepathic dreams and communicate with others while dreaming.) On the other hand, when we're awake, we're actually dreaming a shared space. We're co-creating this space and thus, its persistence. With a solo dream, we know the reality created by the mind is flimsy. But what if the reality created in the waking state is just as flimsy? If that were so, is it possible that we could shift away from the undesirable aspects of our persistent reality by starting to dream a better one with others? That is what we're doing with social meditation and, specifically, the sharing after the journey. In a sense, we're exploring community dreaming, and the sharing of experiences that occur at the edge of our dreams. We're playing back and forth between dreams. The narrative is the dream, a dreamlike meditation, that we're doing in partnership with others. That partnership strengthens the connection between people and gives some elasticity to our sense of reality. We then have more agency within the reality we perceive. We propose that by practicing this type of alternate-reality exploration in five-minute increments, we can strengthen these new neural circuits and rebuild the neural pathways that tell us what reality is—and isn't.

By re-creating our neurology in this way, we have the mechanism to wake up, to become lucid any time we want during the day, and to do so without needing to go into a deep meditative state to access the awakened self. We can actually start to pull ourselves into the awake state permanently or, at least with greater persistence. So instead of a persistent delusion, we start to live with persistent curiosity—ready and willing to investigate what might be true and create a new reality rather than settle for what is.

The Extraordinary World That's Right Beneath Your Nose

In her book, *Extraordinary Knowing: Science, Skepticism, and the Inexplicable Powers of the Human Mind* (Bantam Books, 2007), Elizabeth Mayer recounts a highly unusual experience she had with a dowser. (If the word dowser conjures an image of a person holding two rods in a V whilst looking for underground water or precious metals, you're on the right track. In a spiritual context, dowsing is often referred to as "divining.")

Mayer is a psychoanalyst and a professor in the psychology department at UC Berkeley and the University Medical Center at San Francisco. Calling a dowser to find a lost object wasn't exactly her bailiwick. But her daughter's very expensive and irreplaceable harp had been stolen. After trying everything she could think of and declaring the case hopeless, Mayer became willing to try something she never would have thought of if not for a friend who suggested she put a dowser on the case. So she set aside her skepticism just long enough to call Harold McCoy, then president of the American Society of Dowsers. Not only did McCoy find the harp, he found the house in Oakland, California where the harp was located. It goes without saying that "my dowser told me the harp is at that address," was too flimsy a tip for the police to get a search warrant, so Mayer resorted to posting flyers in the alleged thief's neighborhood. Long story short, Mayer's daughter was reunited with her harp a couple weeks later. Thus began Mayer's fascination with the extraordinary powers of the human mind.

For the next decade and a half, Mayer collected stories (primarily from her colleagues in the field of medicine) and did a deep-dive investigation into what she terms "anomalous experiences." In the late 1990s, Mayer joined forces with Carol Gilligan, Ph.D., a faculty member at Harvard, to convene a discussion group called "Intuition, Unconscious Communication, and 'Thought Transference'" at the American Psychoanalytic Foundation's bi-annual meeting. They wanted to explore these supposedly anomalous (read: "psychic") phenomena with other highly regarded, credentialed professionals. They were totally surprised by a landslide of reports that came crashing in—from patients whose dreams precisely mirrored their analysts private life to spontaneous healings. All of the stories would have sounded bizarre to the average person. But for these clinicians, they were clearly commonplace when taken as a whole. The individuals who heard about or experienced these unusual phenomena were sufficiently unsettled by the experience that they issued a self-imposed gag-order. In fact most of them said, in effect: "I've never told anyone about this before, but... "

Which brings us to the downside — the social, and personal costs and consequences — of disavowing anomalous experiences. It is this downside that we aim to counteract by encouraging people to share what they experience on a Wacuri Journey (or in everyday life for that matter) that they might not otherwise reveal for fear of being labeled "crazy."

Perhaps the best way to illustrate the cost of ducking the issue of non-ordinary realms and experiences is to share a story about a world-class neurosurgeon that Mayer tells in Chapter One of Extraordinary Knowing. This doctor had exhausted the potential physiological causes of his incurable headaches when he called Mayer for a psychological consult. Of their first appointment, she writes:

"... he begins to describe his work. He's passionate about it. He's also supremely successful. When heads of state need brain surgery, he's flown in to operate. His reputation rests not just in the brilliance of his technique, but even more on his astonishing track record. He undertakes one dangerous, life-threatening surgery after another, yet he tells me humbly and with quiet gratitude, 'I never seem to lose a patient.' He has a loving marriage and wonderful children. He can't think of anything troubling him, no obvious unconscious source for the crippling headaches that are destroying his life."

Looking for a hidden psychological cause of the headaches, Mayer asks the surgeon if he's teaching residents as is typical of doctors at a major university hospital. His answer gives her the clue she needs. Again, long story short (you really must read Mayer's book) the doctor's headaches began the very day he resigned from teaching. His reason for resigning? He didn't feel he could — in fact, felt he couldn't — tell the truth about the unusual "technique" that ensured his 100% success rate in the operating room. Again, quoting Mayer:

"... slowly, reluctantly, the surgeon tells me what he's never told anyone. He can't teach anymore because he doesn't believe he can teach what he's really doing. He tells me why his patients don't die on him. As soon as he learns that someone needs surgery, he gets himself to the patient's bedside. He sits at the patient's head, sometimes for 30 seconds, sometimes for hours at a stretch. He waits for something he couldn't possibly admit to surgery residents, much less teach. He waits for a distinctive white light to appear around his patient's head. Until it appears, he knows it's not safe to operate. Once it appears, he knows he can go ahead and the patient will survive."

For this surgeon, the white light above his patients head amounts to an impossible dilemma. If he were to reveal his secret, what would the residents think? What would the dean of the medical school think? You don't have to walk a mile in his scrubs to know they'd think him crazy. So he keeps to himself, shares his special technique with no-one, and endures intractable headaches.

Those headaches are the personal cost to this doctor, but what of the cost to the public? Given the fact that surgical suites around the world are booked all day everyday, the cost in terms of lives lost must be enormous. Imagine the suffering that could be eliminated if all surgeons enjoyed 100% success rates? And this is just one of the thousands, if not millions of ways we cheat ourselves by staying silent about our supposedly "anomalous" experiences.

For Dan Spinner and many others, experiences like these aren't at all unusual. "When I look deeply at this type of phenomenon," Dan says, "they all involve high flow states. That's the common denominator that opens the door to potential futures that would not otherwise appear. I'm guessing this is also what the neurosurgeon is doing, although the way he describes it is a bit different. Once in a state of high flow, I wait until a direct line between me and the individual or group I'm working with is formed. It may take a moment; it may take a couple of sessions. When that direct line is there and is combined with intentional focus toward a goal, outcomes that, by all probabilities, should not readily appear or appear at all, are suddenly right there. They often show up as obvious solutions, as if they were right beneath your nose all the time. The combination of high flow and intention makes what some might call the miraculous absolutely ordinary. The key is to trust the amazing powers of the human mind in a state of flow."

Chapter Seven

From Flatland to Wonderland

Alice Bailey (1880-1949) is perhaps the most widely published of the theosophists. Dan began reading her books in the early 90s and still has many of them on his bookshelf. When he first tried to read Esoteric Psychology and The Soul, he found himself scratching his head and asking, "What the heck?" Reading Baily was 90% tedious, and 10% exhilarating, but he puzzled his way through. Bailey's writings were, to his way of thinking, extremely obscure and difficult to comprehend. He sensed there was a something to what she had to say, but just what she was trying to get across was far from obvious. Nonetheless, he loved those books. They were like talismans. He still has those texts 30 years later. Nowadays, he finds 90% of the material exhilarating and only 10% tedious. From a place of inner knowing and wholeness, having stable access to a state of high flow, he better comprehends exactly what Bailey was pointing to in her writing. Every line makes perfect sense.

Isn't that interesting? Spinner was curious enough to bring Eastern and Western traditions together (through Aikido and Theosophy) in a way that worked for him in both his personal and business life. He followed his hunger to know, pulled from various sources, and was able to make sense of that which cannot be said or fully understood with the mind alone. That's what we are encouraging you to do. Find your way into a state of high flow, however you may get there.

The known and the unknown

When you're in a state of flow and curiosity is at its height, there is something utterly exhilarating about the unknown. Unfortunately, most of us find it uncomfortable to hang out in not knowing for long. We tend to jump to conclusions out of a need to know and be seen. When we do so, this movement of mind chatter deadens the moment.

"In any one day there are moments where there is nothing going on, but we link up what is happening from thought to thought without any space. We overlook the spaciousness that it's all happening in."

~Gangaji

Even when we carefully examine a situation to arrive at our conclusion, that mental exercise can take us out of the state of wonder characteristic of not-knowing but still seeking.

Sages throughout time have advised: "Have no opinions." More often than not, our conclusions are derived from our opinions. We map the unknown onto the known by referring to the past. In so doing, we reinforce previous opinions and assumptions. We often use what's occurring in the now to verify previous assumptions as well as our conclusion and choice of action about what is happening. In this way, we support decisions we've already made and thus hold the position we've adopted. Our ideas get collapsed with our sense of self. This process happens lightning fast, outside of conscious awareness. The net result? We tend to become over-identified with our opinions, decisions, and positions. This internal feedback loop results in a sense of "self" that is unnecessarily restricted and narrowly defined.

Wake up curious and you begin to live in the question "What if...?" That's when a more unrestricted and open ended self can emerge.

A person who is deeply curious has no strong opinions. More to the point, they recognize their strong opinions and let them go. They have discovered a joyful way of life where the priority becomes simply learning, soaking it all in. This is a state of being fully alive, fully in the moment. Gone is the mind chatter that the petty ego wants and needs.

In the words of Eckhart Tolle, author of The Power of Now:

"Two or more people express their opinions and those opinions differ. Each person is so identified with the thoughts that make up their opinion, that those thoughts harden into mental positions which are invested with a sense of self. In other words: Identity and thought merge. Once this has happened, when I defend my opinions (thoughts), I feel and act as if I were defending my very self. Unconsciously, I feel and act as if I were fighting for survival and so my emotions will reflect this unconscious belief. They become turbulent. I am upset, angry, defensive, or aggressive. I need to win at all costs lest I become annihilated. That's the illusion. The ego doesn't know that mind and mental positions have nothing to do with who you are, because the ego is the unobserved mind itself."

In the Aikido dojo, students are taught to be curious when a 6'4" black belt is coming at them with balled fists rather than react. Curiosity is like a crack in the mirror that otherwise would only reveal two options: fight or flight.

For our purposes, the question becomes: what if neither fight nor flight is the only or even the best response to a potential threat? Is there a state of awareness I could cultivate that would make me more effective in the face of perceived danger?

That is the essential premise of Wake Up Curious.

To enter that state you must be curious enough, present enough, and available enough to feel where your body knows it needs to go. And you can learn to sustain these three qualities — curiosity, presence, and availability — moment to moment to moment. It sounds harder than it is, as you will discover. In fact, you do it whenever you stumble into a state of awe or fall in love.

Before we go further, let's talk a bit more about curiosity.

The kind of curiosity we're talking about gives the ego mind no satisfaction whatsoever. The ego-dominated mind will just scream, "But I want to know." This conditioned need to know has its roots in the illusion of separateness. The egoic self wants to arrive at a place of rest where it can relax and say, "Oh yeah, I understand, okay, I got it." The human mind does that kind of extrapolation automatically. Once we reach the point where we can say, "Now I know what's going on," the mind lets go. You've come to understand that issue or this circumstance — for now. The unknown has ceased to be a threat. Your emotions and their corresponding biochemistry self-regulate. Any physical tension associated with being faced with an unknown dissolves as well. And then there's another moment.

Life is nothing if not constant movement, at all levels.

If you look closely, in our bodies, in our cells, in our relationships, in the stars, in the entire cosmos, all is eternal movement and change. The most adaptive way to surf all of that is to stay curious. Athletes call it being "in the zone." They feel One with the entire universe, or at least with their field of play or team. Whether they're surfing, skiing, riding a horse, or dribbling down the court, they're hyper alert and present to the moment. They are tuned into to the subtlest change in their environment. Likewise their body and their equipment. All that input is feeding them what they need to know to handle what's next. Ask an athlete to describe what it's like in the zone, and they'll tell you their mind is not in control. The same is true of musicians who find their way into "the pocket." The body and mind are very connected, we might even say fused with their spirit.

In that sense, curiosity represents a doorway to the heavens, or what we might call the unseen. A state of high flow can readily follow.

Which brings up a curious aspect of curiosity. You can't think your way into the fullness of the moment. You can't think your way into admitting you know nothing, but you can feel your way into it and surrender to not knowing. In terms of depth and totality of knowing about anything in particular, we know very little. But admitting this to oneself as a thought (or even a thought experiment) is altogether different than having a profound realization that you know nothing (or at least very little) and allowing yourself to be deeply impacted by the feelings that accompany the realization. The new awareness and understanding gained can then carry you over the threshold of a deeper kind of knowing into spaciousness and exhilaration. And while most of us will resist what Buddhists call "beginner's mind" initially, that reluctance eventually gives way to liberation in a place of complete surrender.

It starts with an attitude of "I'm going to become informed, I want to learn more." Curiosity allows us to become like a sponge. The relationship between curiosity and consciousness is one wherein active discovery allows us to absorb the world along with the vast store of knowledge humanity has gained about the world. We learn from others as well as from ourselves through self-reflection. We learn from the environment around us, and from animals. Wherever and whenever we open the aperture of the mind without judgment to see in new ways, we increase our level of consciousness. The natural result is that we are then available to assist others, to partner with them and with our communities, to learn, engage, share and support their consciousness and needs and, in turn, expand our understanding and impact.

Manifesting From A State of Flow

In the flow state, anything you want to happen, can happen. It doesn't happen through the ego; it's about alignment with the higher good. Your own higher good, that of humanity, the higher good of the planet, and of the entire cosmos. Put another way, in a state of high flow, you often simply know precisely how to consciously manifest whatever comes into your attention and intention. As long as what you want to manifest fits certain basic criteria and you maintain a state of high flow, it's easy to stumble into the just-right synchronicities and circumstances, find the just-right partners and just-right opportunities. It's even easy to generate whatever you need in terms of money, energy, and resources, not for your ego but for your higher self and the good for all.

Here's an example of how that works. In the fall of 2018, Dan's wife was in Africa opening a beautiful all-girls school in rural Ethiopia for the poorest of the poor. Dan went with her to get her set up but first spent a week in London. He was wondering how he was going to stay connected to her during her three year contract. Her employers, a foundation headed up by a hedge fund owner in London, got wind of Dan's background. He'd run numerous foundations and had been the VP of several Universities and hospitals. The foundation chair said to Dan, "I understand you've got a substantial nonprofit foundation background."

Dan said, "Yup, why?"

His wife's employer replied, "Would you do me a favor? Would you sit in on my foundation board meeting and just observe and give me some feedback?"

Dan said, "Sure."

After the meeting, Dan gave the man his honest feedback. In his estimation the board members were well-intended, but they were inexperienced and had a lot to learn. The foundation founder responded, "I'd like to take advantage of the synchronicity of you being here. Your background would be of great benefit given where we are now at the foundation. We need your help." They negotiated a comfortable contract and the foundation offered to fly Dan to London regularly to be their strategic advisor. It was simple for Dan to thus travel to London regularly and go on to visit and support his wife in Africa. This was an easy moment of synchronicity and flow.

Flow Transforms Crisis Into Opportunity

We can all do life this way. We truly can live life without the needless struggle, the "unnecessary suffering" most people are weighed down by on a daily basis. You can live your life awake and in flow. That doesn't mean you won't have moments of upset, confusion, difficulty, or even real pain. It's not to advocate for a life of ego-based ease. It is simply to recognize that it is possible to live with more and more ease that serves your higher purpose — if you're determined. If you dedicate yourself to staying alert moment-to-moment, your life will transform. In time you will find that you have ready access to a state of flow. Guaranteed.

In a state of high flow, what would throw waves of upset into anyone's world will cease to register on you as such a serious problem. Consider what happened to Dan when he needed heart surgery. He didn't have any symptoms other than a little shortness of breath. Luckily, he went to his doctor and got it checked.

The doctor reported, "You have three blocked arteries. We're going in; we have to unblock them. If you hadn't come to see me, you could easily have died of a massive heart attack."

Dan had recently reconnected with the writings of Sri Aurobindo and was very connected to his energy field. He was doing a lot of meditation with Aurobindo, what he calls his council of elders, and his guides. He took them with him into the operating room when he got his chest ripped open.

He went into surgery infinitely grateful that he had discovered his condition in time. He'd never had angina. Dan is a diabetic and diabetics don't usually get angina, so he had no way of knowing about the blockages in his heart.

He underwent a triple bypass full of gratitude, meditating every moment he could. Like all patients who have their sternum split open, Dan could barely move after the surgery. He approached his recovery as an opportunity to meditate his way through a difficult situation. He meditated and meditated and meditated, focusing his attention on clarifying his next steps on several key projects.

When he went to see his heart surgeon a few weeks later, she said, "So tell me about your post surgery depression."

Dan said, "Excuse me?"

His doctor said, "Tell me about your post surgery depression. Almost every cardiac patient in my practice experiences severe depression after a bypass."

Dan said, "Well, I'm sorry to disappoint you, but I am not depressed. I never had one second of depression. I can pretend if you want. If it'll make you feel better that you did your job."

The doctor said, "How did you do that?"

Dan said, "I've been meditating for 40 years, which helps. But truly, a person doesn't need to have that background to use this type of experience as an opportunity to journey into the essence of what's most true and real." According to Dan's doctors, his healing and recovery was remarkably rapid.

Even in a crisis, even in a life threatening situation, we can find a state of flow. That's not to say it's easy. Having one's chest pried open with a rib spreader is far from easy. Flow isn't synonymous with easy, however, being in a state of flow makes even life's biggest challenges less stressful. Clearly, heart surgery is a physical trauma to the body that requires a period of recovery. But the experience is made even harder when we contract mentally and emotionally. So how do we avoid getting contracted? Isn't it normal to worry and feel afraid when faced with a life-threatening situation? Of course it is. But there is an alternative and supra-normal capacities can be learned as Dan's experience demonstrates. It starts with remaining curious, open-minded, present and aware. Cultivate those qualities on an everyday basis and they'll serve you in a crisis. It's perfectly natural to contract your "field" a bit during a life crisis, but you may find yourself more and more resilient, and better able to open your field and find your sense of flow more readily. This is one of the primary benefits of the Wake Up Curious approach.

Curiosity, Flow, and Healing Trauma

The utility of curiosity and flow when confronted with residual trauma or post-traumatic stress symptoms is also worth noting. Consider Dan's relationship with his father, who was both emotionally and physically abusive.

Reflecting back on his childhood, Dan says: "I realized in hindsight that many of the incidents of abuse occurred when I talked about anything that did not match my father's worldview. I was a happy kid living in a friendly universe that was alive and interactive. As I grew older, I came to understand that my father could not or would not enter that world. In fact, it's quite likely he never even considered the notion that he held a particular worldview, much less that his worldview was so narrow it actually limited his experience. I can say with 100% certainty: the possibility that the universe is friendly never occurred to my father."

Despite his father's insistence that he was just doing his job by teaching his energetic son "discipline" so he could grow into a competent adult, Dan came to realize that his father's motivations ran much deeper than that. "My father's rage came from a deep-seated, emotionally shallow, scientific materialist point of view and, as I later realized, his own childhood trauma. Like so many men of his generation, there was no room in his psyche for his feminine side. Emotion was not in his wheelhouse."

Whenever the young, innocent, happy go lucky Danny tried to give voice to his inner experiences — whether talking with trees or walking into a room and just knowing what everyone was feeling — he got in trouble. Big trouble. At first this was terrifying for Dan and terribly confusing. Eventually it became unacceptable as Dan realized that his deep, intuitive connection with everything and his love for life was being mocked and belittled. In retrospect, Dan recognized that the abuse was his father's vicious and often violent attempt to force Dan to acquiescence and conform to a linear view of reality.

Spontaneous Resolution of Trauma

Dan had spent very little time with his aging father for over a decade. A few years before his dad passed away, while he was still reasonably competent, Dan offered to help him on his computer one night. His dad was losing his eyesight. Although he could see, he was legally blind and relied on magnification software. It was hard for him to do Internet searches because, in those days, the magnification software didn't work all that well. But he was excited about buying a new digital camera. Dan noticed his dad struggling to see what was on the monitor and wanted to help out. His father's temperament had grown more and more cantankerous as he got older (even casual conversations often led to an argument), so Dan had some misgivings. Nonetheless, he asked his father if he wanted some help. His father said, "Yeah."

Reflecting back, Dan says: "In order to avoid a blow up, I knew I had to be as caring and fully present as possible to support him."

The two of them had a great couple hours of intense effort. True to the engineer he was, Dan's father wrote up all the details on the various features of different models. Finally, he selected a digital camera. As soon as they were finished, he put down his notepad and stood up. He went outside to have a cigarette and came back a couple minutes later. He looked at Dan and said, "So I guess that's how you bullshit all your clients."

It was a familiar refrain, one Dan had heard throughout his life, but he was stunned that his dad was mocking him for helping him do something he'd been struggling to accomplish on his own.

"I was crushed," Dan says. "And enraged. I'm not a violent man, but I'm a black belt and could've flattened him with one finger. It was one of only two times in my life I felt that kind of intense anger rise up and felt close to becoming violent. After all those years of physical and emotional abuse when I saw no choice but to just take it, here it was again, right in front of me."

Dan had to use all his skills of centering to stay calm, in spite of the rage he was feeling. He stood up, drew a deep breath, got right in his dad's face and said, "No dad this is just me loving you."

His father was stunned. For once in his life he didn't come back with a sarcastic smartass comment.

"His eyes widened and he just stood there. The moment of high tension and eerie silence that followed seemed to stretch out for a year. I saw him as a three year old. I knew his mother, my grandmother, and realized he had never known love from her. I saw the whole history of my family, the intergenerational dysfunction, how it influenced the way my father treated me, and I realized that it was never about me. It was about his pain, his disconnection and lifelong trauma. Suddenly, I knew his pain in my own body. My heart broke open and I forgave him. I didn't say so out loud—he wouldn't have understood—but in the silence of my heart, I forgave him completely."

For Dan, that very personal, quiet moment brought "instant" transformation wherein all of those years of terror, confusion, and loneliness suddenly transmuted into love.

"But it wasn't exactly instant, more like the cumulative trauma coming to a peak," Dan says.

This kind of cumulative awareness leading to a moment of transformation is not uncommon for those involved in personal growth work. You've likely experienced this kind of radical change in perspective at an intensely personal moment yourself. It can happen in a moment of high tension or a moment of profound awe.

In Dan's words, "Regardless of my challenging childhood, or perhaps because of it, I learned to trust my inner knowing. That innate sense I had as a boy—that there is a loving connection between and among all things—never ceased to inspire me. And it only grew stronger over time. It has become the guiding principle in my life and work. Not surprising, it is also a major theme in our efforts to help people Wake Up Curious."

The Democratization of Spirituality

We make what some might regard an outrageous assumption: that everyone is their own teacher and guru—even their own saviour. Our aim initially is simply to awaken the individual to this as a possibility, then as a lived experience and, ultimately, as an alternative reality of their own choosing. Over the centuries, most spiritual practices and wisdom traditions have been hierarchically structured and controlled by patriarchy. While we honor the essence of those traditions, we also advocate for the democratization of spirituality. To that end, we are offering an approach that is radically and deceptively simple, one that offers dramatically more access to one's Inner Wisdom.

The key, or access doorway if you will, is in the shared resonant field, which is invoked and enlivened by transmissions. This ancient concept cuts across many centuries, cultures and spiritual practices. Typically, a transmission is directional from teacher to student or guru to disciple. We have revised that methodology and reformulated transmission by taking the essence of the transmissive act, offering it live, reproducing it in recorded form, then making those recordings available to anyone who wishes to receive, share, sense, or feel the transmission. When they share in a transmissive atmosphere within a group field, people feel safe and are able to be "seen." They become more open and vulnerable to themselves and others and thus access more of their own healing insights and flow.

Different people experience this in different ways at each moment and in each of the hundreds of recorded journeys. What they receive and what they do with it depends entirely on their level of awareness, and is deeply influenced by their "story"—how they hold or interpret their personal history. Despite these differences, people tend to share any number of comparable moments with others after a given journey. This is revealed again and again in the dialogue that follows the journey proper. In practice, the group-share extends the resonant transmissive field created during the Journey. What's more, it does so on two levels: with the particular group that just went on the journey, and within the larger community of listeners who have taken the journey in the past and will take it in the future. In other words, participants share their wisdom and add it to the wisdom swirling around in the collective consciousness, thus pooling their learning at a higher level of reality. That state, or resonant harmonic pattern, can then be accessed more and more through practice.

Hopefully, this discussion has given you a sense of what we mean by "the democratization of spirituality." It's the process of gaining the tools, practices and empowerment to discover and live your own Truth rather than someone else's.

Creative Teams and Flow States

Henry Poole and his executive team at CivicActions are very intentional about creating an atmosphere that allows creative teams to enter a state of flow. Of utmost importance is to create an environment wherein team members are relieved of worry and stop being concerned about whether they are right or wrong. This allows for the energy of the team to move and gain momentum, because the threat of failure has dropped out of the equation. "It's amazing what happens when people feel no need to defend their opinions," says Henry. "I'd even go so far as to say this type of environment is a pre-condition for flow."

Dan Spinner agrees. "Nothing stops the flow as quickly as someone holding to a strong opinion or trying to prove him or herself," he says. "When those habitual stances dissipate, ego-attachment starts to dissolve. And when the ego recedes, people start to feel the flow of the universe. That puts them in an open-minded, vulnerable, open-hearted state where they are less likely to overthink things. They can simply allow the creative energy to go where it will, moving everyone toward their shared goals. This, in turn, supports group effort because it becomes obvious to everyone that the team as a whole is greater than the sum of the individuals involved."

You might ask: "How do I create such an environment for my teams? Is there a specific method or approach that readily gets people into that state?" Excellent question. Especially given how often teams get bogged down under pressure to perform or get it right.

At CivicActions, they've developed a highly effective practice to help everyone in the company be present in the moment. Becoming present is like hitting the reset button, letting go of whatever is in the way of flow. They have done this by institutionalizing what they call balance scores. Here's how it works: everyone in the company is encouraged to know and honor their priorities. This isn't always easy; people tend to assume they know their needs and desires when, in actuality, the specifics are vague. As long as a person's priorities are vague, they will find it difficult to maintain balance. In Henry's words: "We start out by having our employees identify their needs in three domains: personal (relationship to self and other as well as one's body), professional (this includes a person's specific career and work-related goals), and spiritual (this includes our connection to something bigger than ourselves). These are personal; we don't ask them to share them, just to constantly re-assess and pay attention to how well they are in touch, each moment, with their personal priorities. We ask them to assign a number from 1-10 on how well they know these priorities."

"Next, we ask them to share how well, in the current moment, they are honoring those priorities using the same scale of 1-10. There is not a right answer. We don't expect people to maintain perfect balance. We ask them to average those scores into a number between 1-10 and share the number with their colleagues in our daily meetings. There is no expectation to share any details. It's just a simple reminder that we each have the power and responsibility to honor our individual needs."

According to the best practices established within the company, employees do this by asking questions of themselves such as: "Am I paying attention to my body?" "Am I attending to my relationships?" "Am I making progress toward my aspirations and professional goals?" It's a simple process, but the effect can be powerful. The practice is an invitation to honor priorities, which affords the individual a direct route into the present moment where they can find more balance. When in a state of balance, the flow state becomes more accessible. This practice of checking in with oneself can be done alone but is often done with colleagues.

"We almost always do personal check-ins during our meetings," Henry explains. "The more we can learn to focus our attention, be present in the moment, let go of trying to prove we're smart, creative, empathic, the less we feel separate from others and the more readily we can get into a state of flow. Some of us use balance scores at home with family members and loved ones to course-correct when we're feeling out of balance. We do it with our government clients. It's been incredible to watch clients pick up the practice and start to apply it in their work environment."

Another important convention that is well established at CivicActions is forthright and direct communication. In practice, this involves two principles. The first is simple: no third party conversations. Employees don't talk about a colleague behind their back, and they only say what they'd say directly to the person. The second principle is about withheld communications or what is often referred to simply as withholds.

Henry explains it this way: "When I withhold a tension or appreciation from another, I sacrifice the connection with that person. Plus, withholds tend to feed resentment. If someone says or does something that triggers me — it can be as simple as rolling their eyes — I immediately get defensive. It's a knee-jerk reaction that happens in a flash because I have immediately assigned some meaning to what they've said or done. I may feel offended and before I know it, I'm running a story — a program. It's typically a default program that worked in the past by helping me survive. But in the present situation that old program creates disconnection. I may feel unloved and unappreciated because I think another person has made me wrong. I disconnect even further by making them unlovable, labeling them an asshole or something of the sort. When I take the stance that something's wrong over there and I've been made wrong over here, I reinforce a paradigm of separateness."

The key to aborting the old program is to become curious and aware, to note one's thoughts and feelings and ask, "Is it really true? What else might be true? How else can I interpret what just happened?" How can I use this situation to strengthen my ability to witness rather than react? This pure witnessing immediately brings us back to the present moment. Once present, we can communicate, which immediately reestablishes the connection. We can say, "Ouch! I'm feeling defensive and my heart began racing." At that point, we enter into a loving state in the here and now. And from there, we can find our way back to a state of flow. We're no longer separate. The paradigm of separateness gives way to a paradigm of connection, which is really a state of lovingness. That, in turn, creates affinity and opens a channel for non-verbal communication, an energetic flow state where we feel one with another.

Leadership to the Nth Degree

"The best leaders know how to follow," says Henry Poole. This may sound counter-intuitive at first. But if you take it up as an inquiry and get a little curious, you may discover the best way to develop leadership skills. According to Henry, once you start to actively practice following, you naturally become a better leader.

Most strong leaders had someone who modeled good leadership along the way. The fact is, we humans learn all manner of skills from people who model those skills. The principle behind this is known as "the model imperative," a term coined by American author, Joseph Chilton Pearce.

It's part of the natural order: we do what our models do. More often than not, we are mimicking the behavior of others. We do what they do, not what they say. We don't mean to imply that people never act in spontaneous ways that are more or less original. But it's important to understand that we all have an inbuilt tendency to template off the behavior of others—for better or worse. If you watch little children, it won't take long to see how the model imperative plays out. Parents, teachers, grandparents, aunts and uncles witness this phenomenon all the time. They watch with amazement at how kids seem to "learn by osmosis". Children simply absorb and mimic whatever they see being done around them. Studies show that 95% of what children learn is a direct response to interactions with their environment, which includes their adult models. This stands in stark contrast with the 5% of learning that occurs as a result of verbal teaching or instruction.

It's curious to note that the model imperative remains active once we reach adulthood.

One of the greatest models throughout time once said: "Become like a little child". In other words, be teachable. When you meet someone you admire or stumble upon a person you can look up to, that's when you want to become a learner. Do so intentionally and consciously by watching them closely (without being intrusive, of course). See what they do. Pay attention and let them show you how it's done. Then allow your innate intelligence to take over. You may be surprised how readily you acquire new skills, or hone the skills you already have.

There are as many ways to lead as there are leaders. For example, how do you lead a car from the East Coast to the West Coast when there are so many different choices to make along the way? A leader who prefers the direct route will choose to stay on the highways, whereas another leader will choose the scenic route. Still another will insist on taking the extra long way around so they can stop at each and every body of water along the way. Some people will choose to do most of the driving at night, whereas those who see better during the day will look for a motel or campground as soon as the sun goes down. Each person has a different pattern. Each person's path will be based on their unique preferences, skills, knowledge, and leadership style. And their style will evolve over time.

One perspective holds that the qualities that make for strong leaders are God given, that a particular person essentially has "the gift." From this point of view, one can look at a group of people and pick out the leaders. These are the folks who get labeled "natural born leaders." (There may be something to this, of course. But whether it's a matter of being born with it or having had a good model early on would be hard to assess.) We take issue with this approach and, in fact, see everybody as a leader. We don't take the assertion that "some people have it, while others don't" at face value and assign only those who seem to "have it" the leadership roles. Rather, we give all who are curious (or even mildly interested) an opportunity to explore their leadership potential. We do so by giving them a chance and enough safety to learn.

Consider for a moment the behavior of ants. All ants are inherently curious. They wander around, seemingly aimlessly. What isn't so obvious is that they always leave a trail. Their wandering and curiosity is optimized for finding food. When they do, they go back to the nest or anthill. The others then follow to the source of food. Thus the trail of ants to the pie crumbs left on your counter. All of the ants have this innate ability to lead, and all of them take turns leading and following.

Henry and a few of his friends decided to take this approach when they formed their men's group. All of the group members were strong, smart men who held leadership roles in their lives. A couple of them were coaches, most had created organizations, several had started businesses. In Henry's words, "They were basically alpha males who assume it's up to them to lead." But the men did something unexpected when it came time to architect the group. They decided to create a circle and have a leaderless group. They adopted only one rule: that they would show up and fully commit to being in the circle. Their agreement allowed for the occasional absence when other obligations took precedence, of course, but the point was to bring their full attention, body and soul, to the group. Every man took turns leading an evening. Whoever did had complete control. He would determine the agenda, activities, and direction of the meeting. And while Henry sometimes found it hard to sit there and let someone else run the show, that's when he learned the most. He learned what it was like to follow and, in so doing, discovered more about what it means to lead. He also discovered and reinforced the value of curiosity in a shared collective approach. This is exactly what happens during the sharing after a Wacuri Journey.

Creative Problem-Solving in Flow

If you are a curious person seeking your own higher flow, everyday problems are far less likely to stop you in your tracks. It will be all but impossible to get slowed down by self-pity, sadness, remorse, or depression. Your curiosity will crowd out those states of mind. There's simply no room for them when you look at a situation as a new challenge perfectly suited to your abilities. If you find yourself going nose-to-nose with a vexing problem or suffering emotionally or psychologically, one of the best strategies to shift into a more adaptive mode is to get curious with a clear intent to shift your energy. Look deeply at the problem or witness suffering with a curious attitude and you will see light and movement that would be invisible to you otherwise.

Curiosity brings us into the moment. It brings us right up to the edge of something fluid and moving that we naturally want to soak in. The mind naturally enjoys this type of learning focus. The enjoyment is derived from knowing you're going to learn something new. The moment becomes fresh and open. Then you move on and, again, are in a state of not knowing. When you step into the unknown, you're not in control. But you do get in touch with a deeper truth beneath the illusion of control. We delude ourselves into believing control is even possible in a world that is ever-changing, always on the move, and utterly unpredictable. That deeper truth, that you're not in control, isn't the terrifying chaos the mind makes it out to be. Quite the contrary. That deeper truth holds absolute freedom.

Let's go back to the example of an athlete for a moment. Let's say you're a surfer. Few places are as full of unknowns as the ocean. Tides, waves, undercurrents, the changing winds—all are governed by forces far more powerful than you. Other surfers is another factor. As much as you abide by the Surfer's Creed, "Give Respect to Get Respect," you cannot control what the person on the board 20 feet away from you will do. Nor can you know when a rogue wave might come barreling into shore. But none of that matters when you're in the zone. Even though the waves are clearly chaotic and beyond your control, you experience a feeling of harmony. It's that sense of being "at one with the sea" that keeps a surfer hooked.

A surfer's mindset is one of acceptance of that which cannot be controlled. Rather, they are focused on the feel of the swell as it approaches, and the power of it beneath the board. Meanwhile, they remain aware of the surfers nearby. But they have no need to know anything beyond that, only to surrender to the moment and stay curious and alert. That allows them to enter into a state of high flow. Wacuri can help us to better learn to surf through life.

Curiosity is endemic to the state of high flow.

Curiosity can be profound, sublime, silly, and fun. There are a thousand ways to learn and a thousand entry points that invite us to "go with the flow." A key marker is when your curiosity is aroused and you feel a sense of delight and surprise.

Curiosity In Organizations

Our curiosity not only takes us to a state of flow within ourselves, it can also spill over into our organizations. Let's take a look at some of the benefits of curiosity and resultant flow within organizations. From time immemorial, humans have organized themselves in groups to accomplish specific tasks. For our evolving antecedents, the tasks at hand were those of hunting and gathering. Women would gather together in groups to collect edibles from the forest. Men would organize themselves in hunting parties when going after large game. Organizations also existed in the royal houses of Europe. For thousands of years and up to this day, their homes have featured a sizable staff carefully organized to fulfill certain roles. Whether it was a lady in waiting attending the queen or a groomsman tending the horses, each individual has a designated "station" within the organization. The organizational chart at any given castle or manor of old would be similar in design to all the others. Most, if not all, had a formal structure that clearly outlined who was responsible for what, who reported to who, as what the consequences would be for failure to perform one's duties. The relationships between all members of the household would be clearly defined, right down to the proper manner in which those with a title or managerial position (the "superiors") were to be addressed by those below them (their "inferiors"). Perhaps the household even had an operations manual and organizational chart of one sort or another. More likely, however, all the regulations and controls were traditional and so well-established in people's minds that they were simply understood.

Likewise, businesses have historically been built around some type of formal organizational structure. A formal structure outlines what we, in today's world, might refer to as "best practices." These include a specific set of guidelines and recommendations that come down from the C-suite and are implemented by management. All those within the organization, from senior managers to janitors, are expected to adhere to these guidelines when conducting business, both internally and externally. Some businesses develop flexible elements to their structure. Nevertheless, formal structures exist within most businesses in one form or another.

There is, however, a downside to these types of formal structures. People tend to create organizations and think about them as if they are dead. The CEO and vice-presidents will design an organizational chart but fall short of breathing life into it simply because they don't see it as alive. On the other hand, organizations that are flexible are full of life, even messy. Members of the organization can sense this and feel the flow inherent within it. Information moves freely throughout the organization. Employees might exchange roles and, in so doing, support each other to fulfill their responsibilities. They might even be rewarded for demonstrating an ability to "go with the flow" and adapt to changing conditions. In this way, everyone has permission to be curious and inventive, to explore the best way to serve the organization's goals like some of the new practices in high-tech companies.

To our way of thinking, a flexible, curiosity-based organization is closer to nature. You might even call it an "organizational biofield." An organization that lives this possibility may have an easier time creating and maintaining the holy grail of a "positive culture." Such a culture lends itself readily to insightful problem-solving, creative teamwork, and a stronger, more productive organization overall.

As humans, curiosity and adaptability is our natural way of being. We would never have survived millions of years of hominid evolution had we not been adaptable creatures, ever alert to better ways of going about our everyday business. Those better ways reveal themselves far more readily when we are curious, when we see reality as alive, aware that life is a constant flow of energy. Of course, this type of awareness grew out of the cognitive revolution and was not available (or only minimally available) in bygone days of old. But more and more people of today are able to tap into flow in a way our ancestors could not have imagined. Unless, that is, they were fortunate enough to have some form of esoteric training.

For example, in the Arthurian legends, a man — even a king — could only receive esoteric training if schooled by a wizard such as Merlin. Until very recently in India, only men of the priestly Brahman class had access to teachings of the lineage traditions that afforded them full understanding of ancient scriptures, the Upanishads or the Bhagavad Gita. Similarly, Taoist priests were the exclusive recipients of the type of esoteric training that allowed them to apprehend the subtle flows within the energy body that we moderns have accepted as acupuncture meridians. To this day, Taoist teachings maintain that there is a universal life force, the Tao, which flows through and binds all persons and things. For a large segment of the population — those without esoteric training — this is little more than an ideation. It does not live in them as a reality. Consider ancient China, going back 7,000 years, before Chinese culture was so deeply influenced by the teachings of Confucius and Lao-Tzu. The ancient Chinese personified aspects of nature. They worshipped concepts like "wealth" or "good fortune" with religious fervor (an indication that, to some degree, they grasped the notion of flow). Such practices are still alive in China today. It's interesting to note that religious fervor is a close cousin to what we now call a meme, an infectious idea that spreads from person to person throughout a culture. Sadly, memes, like religious fervor, rarely afford the individual depth of understanding and therefore offers little in the way of transformation.

All that said, in today's world, it is vital to realize that organizations can be seen as living things, not static formulations. That is what we mean by sensing and feeling into the possibility of organizational, group, or project biofield. If you start from a place of knowing it all and aspire to set up your organization or project for maximal control, you create an environment wherein the individuals within the organization are hamstrung by the structure. They are far less likely to learn and grow simply because the organization has little energy. Historically, big organizations with controlled environments have been successful because they control communication, manufacturing, distribution, messaging, and thus have certain efficiencies. In some cases, an organization will even go so far as to attempt to control an entire population. In so doing, they put the kibosh on curiosity altogether. In contrast, modern healthy organizations thrive when they are alive and adaptive. Members of an organization do best when allowed to be curious, to fully participate, to constantly learn in order to meet the requirements of a world that is constantly changing. In the tech world, an incurious organization will falter in the face of disruptive technologies. A curious organization, on the other hand, will leap ahead, spurred on by competition, undeterred by breakthroughs or competitors. Rather than shut down they will go into a flow state of deeper inquiry. By design, a curious/flexible organization has the ability to climb up and stand on the shoulders of whatever emerges in their sector or appears on the horizon of the marketplace.

You might ask, "How do I create flow in my organization or project?" We can offer a general recommendation in the form of a metaphor. Creating shared flow is a bit like building a campfire. One must start with an understanding (even a rudimentary understanding) of energy. Then you gather the needed materials to start a fire. You make sure to set the fire where it can get enough air and, at the same time, have enough protection from wind to remain contained. Every step of the way, you must remain curious, which allows you to be in a direct relationship with the fire. The Wacuri Method is an excellent way to develop a relationship with anything; a fire is no different from a board of directors or a senior staff team, if you can achieve a high state of flow. You see, it's the relationship, the give and take of the feeling, the energy, that is the essence of flow. Being in relationship with the natural world (which is always in flow) is how we humans have been able to harness the powers of nature throughout time.

In the words of Teilhard Chardin (slightly edited for our purposes):

"Once we have mastered the wind, the waves, the tides and gravity, we will harness the power of flow. Then, for the second time in the history of the world, man will have discovered fire."

The Wake Up Curious Community

The fundamental assumption of the Wacuri Method is that we are all deeply connected on many levels. This stands in stark contrast to the disconnected way of living and being that is the baseline for so many people. In that sense, the method provides and antidote of sorts, and is an invitation to a "new normal" wherein we feel intrinsically connected to the larger whole. When we remember and actively experience this truth, we make an essential life-affirming shift that impacts every aspect of our lives. This shift is what gives the method its power.

Our interconnectedness, the latticework of all of existence, is far more extensive than we can even begin to imagine. Journeys, along with the sharing afterward, give participants a chance to explore that variety and depth in bite-sized, digestible chunks. These explorations ease the tension that arises from living with the contradiction of feeling separate when, in reality, we are all deeply connected in Being.

When we experience the higher, multidimensional aspect of what we truly are, we find comfort and a sense of familiarity that is often quite revealing. In other words, we are not strangers to this knowing. We may not experience it regularly, but when we do, there is a sense of coming home. We step out of the drama of personality stress and effort and momentarily suspend the inevitable trials of trying, and often failing, to live an impeccable and "successful" life. What often gets revealed in that suspension, that deeper way of knowing, is the many ways we get hoodwinked by the illusion of separateness. We act in ways that may be expedient but reveal themselves as unwise and ultimately ineffective over the long run.

The Wacuri Method is an invitation to participate in a more conscious community. Together with others, you are invited to step into your deeper being, reorient the personality, and get curious as to what that reorientation can mean for your life vis-à-vis your relationships, your dreams, and your everyday issues and concerns. When humans come together to explore in this way, they raise one another's energy level in a mutually-resonant, shared field of intentionality and aspiration. This resonant field can multiply and expand quite rapidly, providing real-time positive "biofeedback" that reinforces this higher state. The Wacuri Method amplifies this resonant field in individuals and groups, encouraging others to Wake Up Curious like a benevolent infection that sweeps through the group mind.

CHAPTER EIGHT

FROM SOLO MEDITATION TO CYBER-SANGHA

It goes without saying: we live in a time of great stress and conflict. Day-to-day life can feel like a compression chamber. At times life's demands can feel a bit like the walls of a giant trash compactor like the one Luke Skywalker escaped in the first episode of Star Wars. It doesn't matter whether the walls closing in on us are of a personal, familial, communal, or societal nature. Walls are walls and they block our progress toward our goals if not dealt with effectively.

If we don't want to be crushed by life, we have to find a way to scale whatever wall is placed in front of us. Maybe we decide to burrow under or go around a particular wall. Sometimes a wall is so daunting, we simply have to blast through it. And in some cases, we may decide the best way through is to cut a hole in the wall and install a door.

A Persistent Delusion

All too often, when we're up against a wall, we attempt to simply ignore what's closing in on us, which tends to result in an even bigger problem in the long run. It's all too easy to sleepwalk through our reality. In modern day psycho-spiritual parlance, this kind of coping is known as denial. In biology, it's known as self-protection. It's what we do when we lack sufficient resources to handle stress.

In addition, we are, as a society, quite skilled at self-medicating, distracting ourselves with screen-time trivia, and skimming social media nonsense. A large segment of the population is essentially asleep in a waking, endless dream. And for some, that dream is an ongoing nightmare. We see these people walking the streets in cities large and small. Some of them are in such profound, unresolved distress, they're about to explode. Heaven forbid one of them gets cut off on the highway. And yet, it happens every day.

If you've ever had a nightmare, you will remember having a strong desire to learn how to wake up. It's the same for those whose waking hours are nightmarish. So why is it so difficult to wake up out of a horrible dream? Societal pressures are certainly causal to some degree.

In 2009, 27% of adults in the United States would need to borrow or sell something to pay for an unexpected expense of $400. Hundreds of millions of people live in fear. Millions are living an economic nightmare with all the stress that attends that state. Others are threatened and living in fear simply because of their skin color, who they choose to love, what they believe or the language or heritage to which they were born. However, even in the midst of an actual personal or collective nightmare, we can learn to wake up and "go lucid" in the dream.

It's a great thing to do if you have nightmares. Likewise if you are walking around, experiencing your life or your country as a nightmare. Go lucid in a nightmare and you wake up inside your dream. You don't stop dreaming, but a part of your sense of self becomes aware that the rest of your self is dreaming. You then have the agency to take charge. In the dream, you become aware that "you" are not just a passenger, you are actually the driver steering the dream. In the words of Albert Einstein, this idea that you are the passenger is an "optical delusion of consciousness." Our real consciousness is actually much much bigger. It includes a driver and a personal (even inter-dimensional) GPS. This part of you can transcend time and space. Learn lucid dreaming and you can learn to control your dreams, waking or sleeping. With practice, you can become more lucid in the waking state, put an end to your personal nightmare and even contribute to bringing an end to the collective nightmare.

An interesting side note: Einstein wasn't talking about dreaming. He was talking about those of us who read books in the here and now, in the realm of time and space. Einstein postulated that here and now are also illusions (or delusions) that are very believable precisely because they endure over time.

Unfortunately, it's not that simple to bend time and space in the here and now. It's far easier to learn to wake up in a dream. The persistence of our apparent reality is quite powerful. It's powerful because it is sustained and thus controlled, not by the individual, but by groups of living beings and the collective consciousness that interprets reality for most of us. In contrast, when we dream, we can learn to be completely in control. But while we are awake, we have other living beings around us, including plants and animals, as well as our fellow humans. Like it or not, their power matches our own so their dreams (or nightmares) are almost indistinguishable from those of each of us individually.

This book is designed to give you a place to begin your own journey and find others to join you in developing the ability to go lucid while you are awake. That's why we call this approach "waking up curious."

Of course, most of us see small fragments of waking up while we are in the here and now. You may have noticed such occurrences throughout your life. We notice synchronicities, like when a friend calls exactly when we were thinking about them. Or when we run into the right person at exactly the right time. These dreamlike synchronicities aren't random. They can actually be programmed into our consciousness much like a computer is programmed.

Meditation and prayer are the most common ways we can develop more high flow and invite more synchronicities. If you desire to experience this more often in your life, this book is for you. It is designed to rewire your neurology such that you can tune into and enjoy more of the synchronicities that happen all around you all the time.

Our goal is to provide you tools to help you wake up and stay awake all day. To, in Einstein's words "reach the attainable measure of peace of mind."

The Better Part of Ourselves

We are not always taught how to form deep and lasting connections, and yet we yearn for them. Collectively, we tend to forget the better part of ourselves, what others have called our better angels. To compound matters, most people have an inkling that something vital is missing but can't quite grasp what it is. There are also those who are acutely aware that they don't have what they need to flourish. These acutely aware individuals tend to fall into two general categories. They either suffer the fact on a daily basis, or they let their suffering become an opening, a gateway into the general trend toward conscious awakening.

Those who are waking up, quite naturally become curious about all and everything around them. They know in their bones that each of us needs and deserves a richer, better, safer, and more meaningful experience in our lives. So, too, do our families, friends, and communities. In this sense, the movement toward conscious awakening has an "all for one and one for all" theme running through it.

If you are reading this book, quite likely you are among the millions of people who are part of this movement. You may even be offering your skills and expertise to those around you to better their own path of growth, health and fulfillment. You may be or hope to be a personal growth practitioner, a yoga instructor, meditation teacher, healer, therapist or a coach, dedicated to waking up and helping others do the same.

It is our conviction, that waking up to our natural curiosity gives us ready access to our better angels, to our higher and best self, and to the world around us. This aspect of who we are is always there, full of awe and wonder. This aspect of who we are is less susceptible to becoming overrun by misery, confusion and uncertainty.

There is no greater goal than to relieve the suffering of self and others and foster a better world. Thus the power in the simple phrase, "the highest good for all." There has never been a time in human history wherein the higher good is more needed and, simultaneously, more possible.

This is the invitation inherent in the Wacuri Method. We invite you to join us on a journey to the possible.

Not Exactly Mindfulness or Meditation

The Wacuri Method shares much in common with mindfulness and meditation. And while these two practices are similar and support each other, they are nonetheless quite distinct from one another. Both are profound paths to well-being and peace of mind. But the two terms are often used to mean the same thing. The fact that they complement each other and often overlap makes it perfectly understandable that people get confused about the difference. They're two sides of the same coin — each has its own specific definition and purpose. So let's double down and get clear on the distinctions, the specific definition and purpose of each.

Mindfulness: This is the practice of simply becoming aware, noticing your thoughts and feelings. You practice paying attention to your behavior, your surroundings, your reactions to people and situations. Everything that occurs in your daily life is an opportunity to become more mindful. You can practice anytime, anywhere, whether alone or with other people. Whatever you are doing, mindfulness allows you to fully engage in the here and now — to "show up" as who you want to be rather than who you are when on "auto-pilot" and unaware of the movements of mind.

The practice can free you from ruminating on the past and reacting in ways that don't really serve you. You also let go of projecting into the future, getting tangled up in "what if's" and judging yourself and others as good or bad, right or wrong. You gain access to the moment where you can be totally present, undistracted, and centered in your heart.

As Jon Kabat-Zinn writes In The Unexpected Power of Mindfulness Meditation: "Mindfulness, which includes tenderness and kindness toward ourselves, restores dimensions of our being. These have never actually been missing, just that we have been missing them, we have been absorbed elsewhere. When your mind clarifies and opens, your heart also clarifies and opens."

Mindfulness is a fresh state of awareness that arises when you pay attention in the moment without judging what's happening, or are willing to see and relinquish your judgements. This allows you to touch into core aspects of the mind that can erase feelings of powerlessness and restore sanity for both body and mind in times of stress.

Meditation: This is an umbrella term for various disciplines that help people move toward a higher state of consciousness and deep concentration. Along the way, the practitioner develops a new relationship with mind and, ideally, learns to self-regulate it.

We have various forms of meditation from which to choose. Those that help you become clear and focused in your mind are often referred to as "Clear

Mind" meditations. Others, such as "Open Heart" or "Meta" meditations seek altruistic states such as compassion, loving kindness, and forgiveness. Still other practices utilize the body to develop awareness. These include hatha yoga and walking meditation. Sound meditations are also quite popular. They include the use of a mantra (sacred word repeated silently), chanting, toning, or tuning into what is known as the "OM vibration" (primordial sound of the universe).

Meditation has a long history as an ancient spiritual practice, originally considered religious in nature, with prehistoric roots that focused on rhythmic chants or mantras. In some tribal cultures, meditation includes drumming and dancing to access altered states. Various forms of meditation have also been part of Buddhism and Taoism for centuries.

The earliest references to meditation are found in the Vedas, the oldest spiritual texts of Sanātana Dharma (translated as: the eternal way) which date back as far as 1,700-1100 BCE. In ancient times, meditation aimed at spiritual growth, a way to transcend negative emotions and attain a state of tranquility. In the 20th century, meditation arrived in the Western World and was adapted to the goals of modern society in both secular and religious contexts.

Nowadays, meditation is commonly viewed as a powerful way to reduce stress and support healthy living. Says Jane Fonda: "I could never still my mind. And then, as I was approaching my seventieth birthday, I thought the time has come. Part of getting older is that as the externals begin to fray so you are beckoned inward. As my mind became quieter in meditation, I discovered this place that seemed to be suspended behind my forehead, like a chandelier hanging from the top of my skull. It was a place of complete stillness."

Imagine being able to find inner peace amidst the busyness of modern life. Or having the ability to calm your frenzied mind when you need to deal with a crisis or even a major disaster. Who wouldn't want that?

What's Unique About the Wacuri Method

Those who meditate alone on a zafu do so in isolation and, ironically, often feel quite lonely. Most meditation apps also involve the individual in a solo endeavor, even though we may be seemingly connected online. Sure, in some apps you can message other meditators and see whose meditating when you are. Nonetheless, the app does not allow you to make a direct connection. In contrast, the Wacuri Method and curious.live platform are designed to connect you directly and immediately with a community of fellow meditators.

Imagine having access to like-minded people who value meditation right there at your fingertips on your mobile device. This is what our curious.live platform makes possible. Our aim is to provide an easy-to-use and readily accessible platform that allows you to meditate with others—anywhere and anytime. You simply go to curious.live on your computer or cellular phone and invite others to join you. You can post an invitation on your favorite social media platform or simply shoot a couple friends a text saying: "Hey! U want to meet me on curious.live for a five-minute guided journey?" Or you can just go to curious.live and join a meditation with whomever happens to show up in the video chat of a particular journey. You and your fellow journeyers start out by going on a recorded journey and, afterward, share your experiences. You see and hear the other people in real time over group video.

Said simply: The curious.live platform makes it possible to join and participate in a cyber sangha.

Yogapedia defines sangha this way:

"Sangha is a Sanskrit word that means association, assembly, company, or community. It was originally used in reference to a Buddhist community of ordained monks and nuns. These days the popular definition has expanded to include all Buddhist practitioners, although the more strict definition from Buddhist scripture applies to those practitioners who have at least directly realized emptiness. In Buddhism, the Sangha is the third of the Three Jewels, along with the Buddha and the dharma (the teaching)."

The word sangha is also commonly used by those who practice yoga to point to the sense of community that arises among yoga practitioners. In various places around the world you can find robust yoga sanghas wherein advanced yogis teach their students, thereby welcoming them into the yogic culture and helping them adopt new lifestyle choices.

In the context of the Wacuri Method, a sangha means a community of deep sharing that expands into the cyber world, lending new dimension and depth to virtual connections. Think of it as a *scalable cyber sangha* that goes with you wherever you go and expands your reach around the globe.

This type of expansive spiritual community is precisely what we have in store for you.

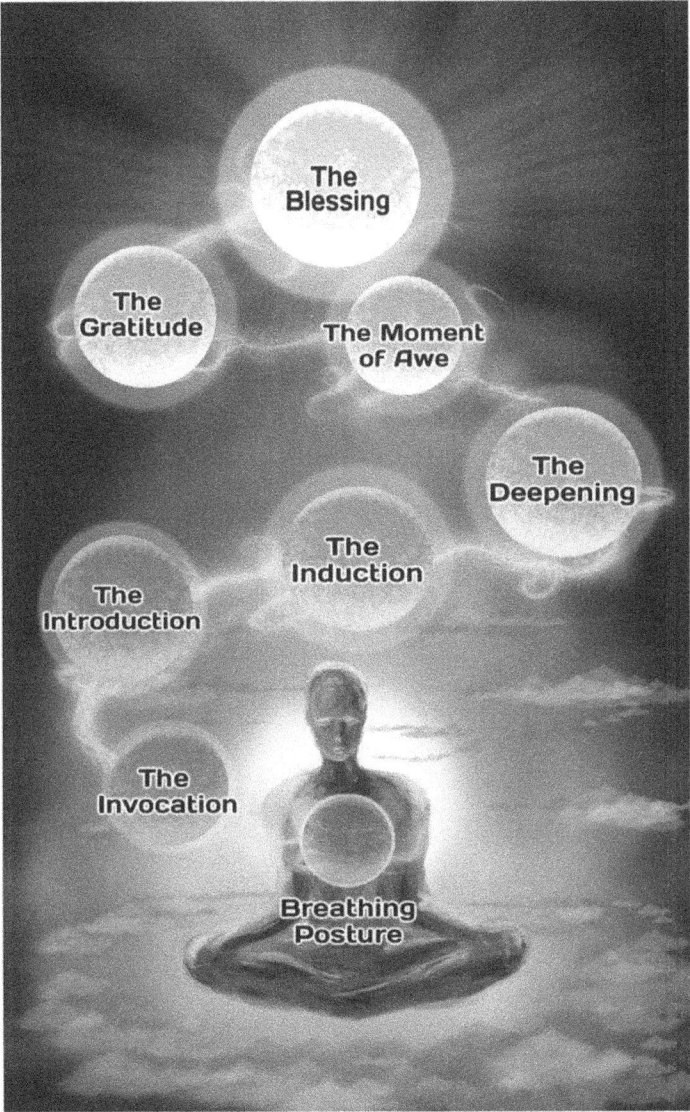

CHAPTER NINE

THE WACURI METHOD AND TECHNOLOGY

Rather than spend our days in a long daydream, dominated by our pasts, futures, to-do lists and responsibilities, the Wacuri Method seeks to wake us up to the awesome possibilities in every moment. A Wacuri journey and the sharing afterward trains you to be present in every moment of your life. It does this by giving you new habits of focus and a witness outside your usual self. The transformative experience of the journey is then made more real because it is affirmed by your co-journeyers in the debrief that occurs when everyone "comes back" from the journey. The meditation is also more intense because it is shared with others. Rather than rejecting society, Wacuri embraces it and asks you to collaborate and connect deeply with each other.

Many Wacuri meditators experience this connection as love.

A Wacuri Journey is always a journey to something which is not yourself. It may be something inside yourself, such as your inner child, your cells, or your relationship with your father. Or it may be a journey to something grand and awesome like a galaxy, or something humble and awesome like a bumblebee. In any case, the ultimate destination of the journey is a moment of awe. A journey seeks to give you an intimate connection to something, like a tree or your dog, and to awaken awe and curiosity from that object. Because the journey is co-created with at least one other person, it always gets you outside your narrowly self-centered self. You and a friend go somewhere, and your experience strengthens their experience, just as theirs strengthens yours. By going somewhere in this way, we begin to realize that we can travel to the essential nature of all things. We begin to have the experience that all is interconnected, all is sacred, and all leads back to Source.

The Wacuri Method

"A lot of people have ideas, but they need to turn them into a diagram or an algorithm or a sequence of steps. One of my skills is doing that. Computer scientists want to know how to do things in ways that can be repeated. I brought that to this team in the sense that I was able to identify and name the elements of the Wacuri Method that Dan and Henry had been doing without naming them," explains Robert L. Read.

Robert L. Read has a Ph.D. in computer science. In his career, he has led a lot of teams focused on creating organizational change using software methodologies to help make companies more agile. He did the same thing in the federal government when he was a Presidential Innovation Fellow. "It's really difficult to create organizational change without also changing culture. So that's part of what leaders in the software field have to do," Robert explains.

Robert believes social meditation can lead to cultural change by changing the way that we think about problems. "Removing ourselves from the minutiae of day-to-day tasks—even for five minutes—can help us keep the bigger picture in mind. When I was in graduate school I practiced Zazen meditation. Often I'd be working on a really hard problem and I would go and meditate. I'd come back and the problem would solve itself," Robert explains.

Rob is a strong believer in psychology. There's a simple psychological theory called social facilitation, which is essentially improvement in individual performance when working with other people rather than alone. A big part of the Wacuri Method is not just the seven phases of the journey, but also the debrief afterwards. The act of saying to another human being, "I felt love or I felt at peace or I was distracted" is valuable to the process. If you say, "I felt like an eagle in flight," you remember the flight better even if those words don't capture all of the sensation and beauty that you were feeling. The act of verbalizing, "I felt like an eagle in flight" makes you remember what it was like on the journey when you felt like you turned into an eagle.

"So I believe—just as Henry emphasized that in lucid dreaming the act of bringing the experience into the verbal part of the brain cements it into the memory—that the experience of meditation is stronger if it's done in the presence of another person, especially when the experience is shared immediately afterwards," Robert explains.

Robert believes that all of us want to be acknowledged and be part of a social structure. The novel, "Invisible Man," about the black man who society doesn't look at and just pretends is not there, is very telling because the worst thing you can do to someone is ignore them, shun them and pretend like they're not even in the room. The opposite of that is to say, "I hear you, I understand what you're saying, and I see you as a human being."

"I think a lot of the problems of loneliness, depression and even substance abuse that we have in our society today can be mitigated by having someone acknowledge you," says Robert. That's why the 'like' button on a Facebook post is important. You want people to like your post or at least acknowledge it. The Wacuri Method offers a much deeper form of engagement. You're not physically in the room, but in a visual chat you're saying, "yes, I understand you felt like a minnow or you enjoy flowers or whatever the situation is. For you to hear me say that has a small but important psychological charge in the same way that a poet is happy when someone comes to their reading. When you have a journey, sharing it and having someone acknowledge it is very powerful to the person that is heard," Robert explains.

I really appreciate the psychological value of you acknowledging my journey even if we might be two thousand miles away from one another. In a guided journey, in the presence of one or more people, it is easier for me to enter a flow state than it is through breath counting in Zazen meditation. I think many people will find it easier to achieve a meditative state of relaxation through these five-minute journeys than if they meditate by themselves sitting in front of a wall," says Robert. The debriefs are often emotional and powerful. Without the debrief, the act of taking a journey exists in isolation. It's more like a dream. It's easier for it to be forgotten than it is if there's a conversation that occurs afterwards.

"Speaking for me personally as a computer scientist and the way I do things, doing this makes me more effective. The five-minute journey and sharing gives me instant relaxation from the oppression of my to do list. For me it lasts about an hour. By doing a journey and being acknowledged and heard afterwards, I feel like I can hold the bigger picture of importance in my mind for an hour. The other benefit of the method, like Henry always says, is that it's easier to workout regularly if you do it with a workout partner. The point Henry is making is that a lot of people want to meditate regularly but they find it difficult to do," Robert explains. The Wacuri Method turns meditation into a social activity. Most people don't want to let their workout buddy down by not showing up if they said they're going to show up. If two people agree to do a journey, there's a certain psychological pressure to show up and be there for your partner. So it increases the probability of forming a habit of doing it if you do it socially.

The Wacuri Journey: An overview

Regardless of whether a particular journey travels into a mundane or exalted reality, ultimately, they all go to the same place. You can go on a Journey to a Slug, or Journey to the Heart of Compassion; either way, you end up at a moment of awe in your own heart.

All our Journeys are delivered spontaneously, unscripted and unrehearsed. However, the Wacuri Method itself has emerged as a structured approach. Paradoxically, this structure gives the journey a tremendous amount of freedom to go wherever it may for both the individual guiding the journey and those going along for the adventure.

The method consists of a series of acts, specifically:

- Breathing and Posture
- Invitation
- Introduction
- Journey Proper
- Moment of Awe
- Space of Appreciation
- The Sharing

These acts flow from one to the other relatively seamlessly over a period of five minutes. In this way, the method compresses an ocean of awe into a small slice of time.

The positive impact of a moment of awe on the human psyche has been the subject of considerable study in recent years (See: APPENDIX D: Additional Resources). When we experience that awe-filled space of wonder, we can better appreciate and live in gratitude for the blessings in our lives. We are also better equipped to cope with life's challenges.

After the journey, the experience wraps up with a process of inclusion and conclusion called a sharing or debrief. This sharing is an essential part of the Wacuri Method; it is the innovation that takes a guided meditation into the new realm of online social meditation.

The Journey Guide

Essential to Wacuri journeys are the Journey Guides, whose formal training in the method or previous experiences allows them to lead a journey skillfully toward the moment of awe. Journey Guides typically have previous professional training as coaches, meditation teachers, healers, or counselors. As with any skilled offering, each individual will be unique in his/her style, depth and breadth of experience, level of awareness, capacity to hold the group, etc. Journey Guide training is available to anyone with a sincere interest in learning the Wacuri Method and offering guided journeys of their own on our platform.

During the first five minutes of a live Wacuri journey, only the Journey Guide speaks. Journey Guides are trained to speak spontaneously from the heart while centered and present. Although many journeys are educational, the Wacuri Journeys are not a lecture; they are meant to be experiential rather than intellectual excursions. Journey Guides are trained to use rich, evocative language to speak to the body, mind, heart, and soul of journeyers. Each journey plays upon different aspects of the human instrument. Some are more intellectual, some more emotional, some more sensual or kinesthetic. The singular "rule" is that a journey is spontaneous rather than scripted, as pre-planning impairs the feeling of aliveness characteristic of journeys. Moreover, a spontaneous journey requires the guide to be fully present, connected to their deeper self, and alive in the moment. This is the very same state they hope to induce in others.

Some Guides prefer to think of themselves as transmitting a journey rather than creating one.

Journey Guides are trained to open up transmission to Source by whatever name they choose to call it. Guides are aware they are simultaneously transmitting the subject matter and connecting with their own version of Source. Whatever name is used, the aim is to co-create the journey with that Source as well as with the participants. Journey Guides always imagine themselves in the presence of the other journeyers traveling alongside them. (This even extends beyond the real-time journey to including future participants of the recording of the journey.) In this way, the journey co-arises out of the shared biofield occupied by the Journey Guide and the listeners, even though the listeners are remotely located and remain silent during the journey.

Now let's consider each Act of the Journey in turn.

Breathing and Posture

Every journey begins with an invitation to focus inwardly and attend to your breathing and posture. A typical opening goes like this: "Be in a quiet spot and take a few moments to adjust your posture and breath deeply. Sit comfortably upright in your chair, or in any posture you can hold for five minutes."

Similar to many meditative practices, the emphasis on breathing is important. The Wacuri Method does not prescribe a specific approach to breathing, it simply encourages participants to begin by bringing their awareness into their own body. This is, in a sense, a point of departure from the workaday world that prepares the participant to downshift, take a break, and set aside five minutes to listen and focus with intention while on the journey.

Invitation and Invocation

The guide then invites the journeyers to join him or her on a journey. The invitation is important; it's a ceremonial element that highlights the individual's choice to voluntarily engage in an activity that is designed to help them consciously evolve. The guide makes no demands on the journeyers; they are free to decline going on the journey. Of course, some participants will engage minimally and listen with a certain detachment, disallowing the possibility of being transported by the journey. Nonetheless, they may benefit from participating in whatever way they can.

A typical invitation goes like this: "Come with me on a journey to… " It can be anywhere from the bottom of the ocean floor to the center of the galaxy to the transmutation of one's deepest fear.

Introduction to Subject

Once the subject has been named, the guide takes approximately 15 to 30 seconds to introduce it. They may appeal to the intellect with a few facts or invoke the natural world with images, or evoke the emotional body with feeling words. Psychologically, this ushers the journeyer into space of the journey and allows them to shift their attention away from their physical surroundings. The journeyer is consciously and with clear intent, making a choice to leave the cares of the day and the world behind. The introduction initiates this process. For many journeyers, it is a welcome relief to direct the mind to move out of whatever thought stream has been flowing (or flooding) through their awareness during the day. This is a phase-shift wherein the individual decides to give their full attention to the guide for a brief time.

The Journey Proper

The Journey proper is a timeless five minutes. That is, the journey should transport the journeyer out of their normal sense of time into a timeless dimension that is characterized by spaciousness. This is "time outside of time." It has a very different quality, a texture if you will, that allows the heart and mind to soar above and beyond the confines of consensus reality. We are temporarily freed from the confines of the conventional world that shrinks us into identity boxes we simultaneously resist and resign ourselves to much of the time.

In some journeys, the Journey to the Inner Child comes to mind, this phase-shift involves a change in psychological position from one of a mature adult with responsibilities to manage, to that of a carefree child full of wonder. In other excursions such as Journey to an Owl, the phase-shift involves a physical journey through the chilly moonlit sky vivisected by pine branches and decorated by the noiseless stroke of a raptor's wings as he extends his claws at the sight of a tasty mouse in the mouldering duff of the forest floor.

Guides maintain their disposition as transmitters of the experience rather than authors of a story. In fact, Wacuri Journeys are not a story because nothing need happen. Nor is it a pastiche, a homage or vignette, because it is not carefully composed. Guides simply listen to their heart and soul and "recite" the journey to the listeners the way a poet or rapper might receive and recite aloud an improvised poem or rap that comes, seemingly out of nowhere.

It should be noted that the guide does not go into a deep trance to transmit the journey, although they do go into a high state of flow. Of course, a part of their mind is still attending to the journeyers and how they might perceive the journey. They might, therefore, make a conscious attempt to enrich the experience by bringing in as many of the senses as possible. And while a Journey to the Beauty of Fractals might not readily lend itself to the sense of smell, the Guide will want to invoke color, movement, and perhaps even sound. In general, the more sensual the journey, often the better.

It is important, however, for Guides to resist the temptation to go overboard and give too much sensory input. Periods of brief silence give journeyers a chance to absorb the transmission and actively generate the sensory experience, thus co-creating the journey in their own minds. The oak tree the journeyer imagines will not be the same oak tree the Guide imagines; the point is for the journeyer to have as vivid an experience as possible by generating it themselves. In radio fiction and other contexts, this inner experience is referred to as "the theatre of the mind." A good rule of thumb for Journey Guides is to pause for five seconds every half minute or so.

The Apotheosis, or "Moment of Awe"

Every Wacuri journey aims to culminate in a Moment of Awe wherein the participants experience a sense of wonder or oneness. They touch and are touched by the Infinite. You might expand beyond your ordinary spatial or temporal frame of reference. It might be a meaning-based frame that essentially gets left behind in a moment of awe. When we are truly awe-struck, everything changes. The change may be subtle, but it's real.

Above all, the Wacuri Method seeks to awaken this sense of awe. The benefit of touching the Infinite can barely be put into words, and is far better experienced than described. It strengthens us on many levels, and that strength can be taken back into the journeyer's everyday life. This affords a rich new dimension to the mundane realities of existence that cannot be captured but only hinted at with words like "awesome" and "epic." A stone is just a stone— until you go on a Wacuri journey and a stone turns into a living entity with an unusual, but undeniable, numinous glow.

Philosophers have been fascinated with the experience of awe since the time of pre-Socratic Greece. So essential is this experience, it is viewed as a foundational passion that drives human culture.

Awe is inspired by a moment of transcendence. Suddenly, our knowledge structures don't make sense anymore. We become speechless, full of wonder. The experience tends to transport us into the vast unknown. Those who have experienced the unknown enough to be comfortable with not-knowing, tend to get curious. But a sudden moment of awe can also give rise to fear. Why? Because when we open to the unknown, it threatens the control of ego.

Say you experience deep reverence and a sense of oneness when you touch the Great Mystery. Meanwhile, in order to deal with the fear, your ego might start scrambling to define and defend it's supreme authority. Wacuri journeys take this into account and mitigate fear by sealing the moment of awe with a sense of gratitude.

The moment of awe occurs at the emotional height of the journey. It is the climax, followed by a moment of gratitude, which allows the journeyer to return to the room. Rather than end with a cliffhanger, the journey culminates in a release of tension, the denouement common to Hollywood movies.

The Moment of Awe is emotionally and psychologically the highest pitch of the journey. It is perhaps the most removed from the need to do the dishes, or whatever "chop wood, carry water" mundane reality the journeyer will return to soon enough. The purpose is not to emphasize the difference between the death of a star and doing the dishes, but to allow the journey itself to infuse life's normal activities with some of the awesome power of a dying star. In so doing, the Wacuri Method encourages participants to appreciate ordinary life and perhaps even experience little moments in time as extraordinary.

A moment of awe, small or large, temporary or extended, can awaken in each of us a renewed sense of connectedness to all living things and all sentient beings, including the deepest aspect of our very selves.

Space of Appreciation

The penultimate moment of the journey is a pause that allows for Gratitude. This may come in the form of finding gratitude in the heart for the gifts brought by the subject of the journey for its revelations. For example, the Guide might say, "When you are ready, come back into the room, give thanks for the wisdom of your inner child and have a wonderful day."

In any given journey, there may be several such pauses, but the most powerful journeys build to a climax of awe and appreciation. This requires space, in the sense that the Guide must pause and allow the journeyers to appreciate the awesome nature of the subject without intruding on the space with their voice. The journeyers should be able to co-create the journey by imagining, or feeling, or thinking, whatever arises spontaneously straight from the heart.

The Return to Everyday Living

Every Journey ends with a brief affirmation of the shared experience and a call to the listeners to gently bring their consciousness back into their body and into the physical space they occupy. It's a blessing of sorts, that celebrates and commemorates what has just occurred and, at the same time, acknowledges that it's time to come back down to Earth and embrace the duties of the day. Hopefully, however, the journeyer will be in an elevated mood, have uplifted their state of mind, and feel more connected inwardly and outwardly on an emotional and spiritual level.

Many journeyers find that this process takes 30 seconds or more. It is often the case that journeyers do not feel moved to speak for several long moments and sometimes, in the case of an intense journey, for quite awhile. In a sense, the gulf between the Moment of Awe and the return to everyday living is so great that it cannot be crossed in an instant. In any case, the crossing must be made intentionally and with awareness of the return as a phase-shift in its own right.

We share this crossing with others who joined us on the journey, returning together from our co-created experience and recognizing the fact that we are two, three, or more people, each sitting wherever we are — in a coffee shop or at the top of a mountain — on a video chat together. A few moments earlier, we may have been three seagulls soaring over the sea, but now we are people with jobs, families, checkbooks, nutritional needs, personalities, and a heavenly host of challenges and problems.

Time to Share

The Share is a signature aspect of the Wacuri Method that allows journeyers to better integrate the experience and harvest the benefits of the Journey and carry them back into their lives. Essentially, they are sharing their common biofield or energy field.

After a moment of suitable length, the Journey Guide asks the journeyers to comment on their experience. Sharing in this format should begin gently and not be rushed. Some journeyers, if there are more than one, will feel an aversion to going first, and some may be reluctant to speak at all. Sharing is invited and encouraged, but not required.

Eventually, someone will want to share what they got out of or learned from the journey. The speaking is important because it is a psychological affirmation that something has just been shared, both for the journeyer and the guide.

As the journeyers describe their experience, they give themselves an opportunity that has immense value, one that is sadly rare in our world: recognition. They are being noticed and listened to. Their thoughts and feelings matter. The group affirms what they hear and, to the best of their ability, understand what each participant feels without judging them.

Some participants will be very cerebral, some kinesthetic, and some emotional. Guides who are comfortable doing so may work with the journeyers and try to elicit an emotional response from the cerebral journeyer for example, or a bodily sensation from the emotional journeyer, and so on. It's important to keep in mind that all ways of experiencing a journey are valuable. It is to be expected that not every person enjoys or experiences each journey equally, and some may not enjoy a given journey at all. Moreover, some people will be more readily transported into the space of a journey than others. It is important to avoid any tendency to turn the journeys into a contest to see who can do the most outrageous antics in the imaginal realm.

The debrief is normally between three and fifteen minutes. It is possible that one person's statement will be a mere fifteen seconds. On occasion, however, the journey will be an intense experience that excites and touches the journeyer, and they will want to discuss it in order to help fix it in their mind.

The Afterglow of a Journey

Let's double down and consider what happens when people share what they experienced during the journey. You need only do it once to register that this is a markedly different conversation from typical conversation (and the polar opposite of chit-chat and small talk). So what is it that's so unique about this form of sharing? First of all, when we feel truly seen and heard, we are far more likely to be vulnerable and open. This allows for surprisingly deep sharing. People who enter a safe space naturally resonate. They simply feel safe, and feel good about themselves and the others involved. True, it's a

small, temporary community, this shared biofield —
perhaps beyond time and space.

People feel, sense, and hear their own humanness
and realize they are not alone. And with others
doing the same, everyone has an opportunity to
become more real and more true. The conversation
that ensues allows for more authenticity, which is
evermore helpful in terms of insights and learnings.
The atmosphere becomes charged. People feel
uplifted and supported. They may experience more
emotional intelligence than they would experience
otherwise. The shared biofield actually calls forth our
better angels. Some psychologists say we can
actually heal ourselves when communicating from
that place. It may well be a key to effective therapy.

Consider for a moment what it feels like in your
body to have an authentic conversation in which you
allow yourself to be vulnerable with someone. Now
contrast that with a conversation wherein you find
yourself putting forward curated impressions, what
might even feel like "false advertising." Most of us
fall into the trap of impression management at times,
certainly in daily life and particularly on social
media. This subtle poison can result in an empty
feeling or make you feel like an imposter. The
Wacuri Method provides an antidote. By design, the
method creates authentic moments between people,

many of whom may not even know each other. In the afterglow of a journey, participants are in a transmissive and receptive state. From that state, they re-transmit to one another when sharing. The transmission thus proliferates and magnifies, creating that resonant harmonic pattern. When you're in a high flow state, that resonant harmonic becomes tangible. Some people can even see it. Those who hear it often call this pattern "the music of the spheres."

A Sample Journey: The Consciousness of Cells

Take a couple of deep breaths in your own rhythm.

Adjust your posture to be comfortable.

Come with me today on a journey to the consciousness of your cells. I want you to imagine cells throughout your body. A few, a lot. One location, several locations. These extraordinarily tiny creatures that hold everything together are one of the critical units of our entire structure.

Imagine your cellular structure, somewhere in your body, everywhere in your body. Millions upon millions of cells. Interacting, sharing information, nutrients in exchange.

And now I want you to imagine that somehow a few of them — just a few — start to light up. In other words, they are aware that you observe them. They lighten up, the light of consciousness. See them perhaps in clusters, in one part of your body or another. Or perhaps many cells, but at least a few. And take a moment now to see your cells lighten up in recognition of you and your growth in your life.

PAUSE
Perhaps now, the number of cells and the location of cells that are lighting up, that are becoming conscious, is increasing. Or perhaps you are aware that their consciousness is increasing. Somehow consciousness begets consciousness. See if your cells now are multiplying their light, feeding one another so to speak, resonating with every light vibration, one to another. Feel your body becoming more alive, more alert, as your cells wake up one by one.

And now these clusters of lit up cells are becoming more and more, almost as if there was a rhythm building in a wave pattern. Feel many more cells lighting up. Somehow connected, communicating with one another.

PAUSE
And now, they are all lighting up. Every single cell in your physical body, lighting up, celebrating you,

celebrating their own awareness, joining you in your growing awareness — bringing health, clarity, strength and beauty. Just sit soaking that up for a moment.

PAUSE

Feel the vibrancy of it all. Reaching a peak. Forever changed. Bright. Bright as you can imagine.

SHORT PAUSE

And when you are ready, give thanks, come back into the room, and have a wonderful day.

END

You have just read a transcript of an actual journey entitled The Consciousness of Cells, guided by Dan Spinner in 2014. The whole journey recording is 5 minutes 17 seconds long. It was performed without a script. Like all such human speech, it is somewhat broken. It is cogent, but does not always use complete sentences. Although the transcript lacks the power of Dan's voice, we hope it gives you an idea of a journey. Keep in mind the content varies quite widely. We hope this encourages you to participate or even try your own.

Note also, that although the journey may be educational to someone who have not heard of the cellular theory of life, it is not intended as a lecture on biology, rather, a visualization that Dan transmits from his own way of experiencing cellular reality directly to the journeyers.

To demonstrate the seven acts of a typical journey, we will now repeat the above journey (in italics), intermingled with commentary on each section or "beat" (in plain text).

Take a couple of deep breaths in your own rhythm.

Adjust your posture to be comfortable.

Note here that Dan directs our attention to our breathing and posture to both prepare for the five minute journey and to bring our consciousness into the body.

Come with me today on a journey to the consciousness of your cells.

The Invitation prepares the journeyer mentally and mentions the subject. The journey may choose to decline the invitation. In this journey, there is no invocation.

I want you to imagine cells throughout your body. A few, a lot. One location, several locations. These extraordinarily tiny creatures that hold everything together are one of the critical units of our entire structure.

Here Dan has introduced the subject, which sets the stage and begins transporting the journeyer out of everyday consciousness and into an imagined space. Note that so far the cells are static—they are not doing anything, they are just there.

Imagine your cellular structure, somewhere in your body, everywhere in your body. Millions upon millions of cells. Interacting, sharing information, nutrients in exchange.

Now the journey is beginning as the cells start to act. The journeyer must use their own imagination to try to picture this.

And now I want you to imagine that somehow a few of them—just a few—start to light up. In other words, they are aware that you observe them. They lighten up, the light of consciousness. See them perhaps in clusters, in one part of your body or another. Or perhaps many cells, but at least a few. And take a moment now to see your cells lighten up in recognition of you and your growth in your life.

The journey now is fully underway. Hopefully the journeyer is completely transported out of the mundane thoughts of their everyday tasks. This journey is richly visual, allowing the journeyer to exercise their own imagination.

PAUSE

To give time to mentally construct this image, the guide pauses. After a respectful time, Dan begins again:

Perhaps now, the number of cells and the location of cells that are lighting up, that are becoming conscious, is increasing. Or perhaps you are aware that their consciousness is increasing. Somehow consciousness begets consciousness. See if your cells now are multiplying their light, feeding one another so to speak, resonating with every light vibration, one to another. Feel your body becoming more alive, more alert, as your cells wake up one by one.

Dan has now brought in a sense of motion and vibration. A somatic component is added with the suggestion to "Feel your body becoming...".

And now these clusters of lit up cells are becoming more and more, almost as if there was a rhythm building in a wave pattern. Feel many more cells lighting up. Somehow connected, communicating with one another.

Although Dan mentions no sound, he invites the journeyer to imagine a rhythmic wave pattern, further enhancing the journey. However, Dan never specifies what color the light given off is. To one, it might be white, to another golden, to another different hues depending on where they are in the body. The guide is not attempting to completely describe the experience, but to transmit ideas and feelings. Here Dan once again pauses before continuing.

PAUSE
And now, they are all lighting up. Every single cell in your physical body, lighting up, celebrating you, celebrating their own awareness, joining you in your growing awareness—bringing health, clarity, strength and beauty. Just sit soaking that up for a moment.

Dan is building to a Moment of Awe. He has brought in an emotion, that of celebration, and the intellectual idea of awareness. Positive imaginations of health and clarity are invited, and then he pauses again.

PAUSE
Feel the vibrancy of it all. Reaching a peak. Forever changed. Bright. Bright as you can imagine.

Dan has now reached the Moment of Awe. He is asking the journeyer to imagine as intensely as possible, and slyly suggesting that this change, which is only been imagined, will outlast the the journey as he says "Forever changed."

SHORT PAUSE
Dan allows the final Space for Appreciation. He gives time for the journeyer to imagine a potentially lasting visual, emotional and intellectual impression.

And when you are ready, give thanks, come back into the room, and have a wonderful day.

This is the Sharing and the Return. Dan gives the journeyer permission to take some time, but reminds them to give thanks. He explicitly guides them down from the peak experience back into the room, which also means into your normal, but perhaps elevated consciousness. Finally, the journeyer is asked to have a wonderful day, a formula which ends the timeless nature of the journey, in which hopefully normal time has stopped, and restarts the journeyers normal perception of time.

Note that this journey might not be perfect. In fact Dan himself scored it an 8 on a scale of 1 to 10. Regardless if the quality of the journey is perfect or imperfect, the key is that the journey be genuine and spontaneously transmitted from the heart rather than scripted. If the journeyers note imperfections in the guide, it enhances the experience in much the same way as a live music performance is more engrossing than a studio performance, even though the studio performance is more carefully crafted and "perfect."

Chapter Ten

Wake Up Connected

Wacuri seeks to awaken people to more flow and presence in their daily lives so they are more aware of what they tend to take for granted. Journeys often remind people of the child-like wonder they once knew. At times, a journey can even restore some of that wonder. This, in turn, revives their natural curiosity, encouraging deeper connections with other people as well as with the objects of their curiosity.

The Impact of the Method

Perhaps the best way to get a glimpse of this is to hear the impact of the method early on, while it was still in development.

This first account is Henry's experience of one of the first journeys Dan led him on in the early days of the method.

"I was a white bird, flying in the sky. I felt light and free and at peace. I saw a large tree in the distance. It looked like a redwood and I flew towards it. As I was landing, I felt myself shape shift into the tree. I felt a groundedness and comfort standing firm and tall in the forest. There were trees all around me. My ancestors and my offspring. I had parents and siblings all around. I had numerous trees nearby that I felt were my children. But I had a sense that they were just extensions of me, like the bird I was. I felt one with everything, but somehow conscious of a kind of separateness. I felt the sun at my leaves and the dirt at my roots. They also felt like extensions of me. As I was experiencing the comfort, I heard a voice in my head. I was being told to listen to the sound of sawing. I realized that a human was cutting down one of my children. I had a sense that I should be angry or upset, but I felt nothing of the sort. In my wisdom, I found myself feeling love for the human — who was also somehow me. I felt a knowing that I couldn't be killed, and that my offspring were not going to be killed by being cut down. I realized that my existence, and that of others is never really threatened.

Light in the Face of Mortality, Wisdom in the Face of Death

This next account from Dan is about the impact of giving a Journey to a group of women with cancer. In fact, this is one of the original experiences that led to the Wacuri Method. In his description we see the impact giving a journey has on the Journey giver.

"It's a warm summer day in a hot, inauspicious, church meeting room. About 30 women are gathered around sitting quietly in a circle. Very quietly. They all have cancer. Some in very advanced stages, others in remission, still others mid-diagnosis or receiving treatment in the agonizing in between time. They range in age from the very young, early twenties, to the seventies. They are very quiet but very present. At the time, I was a Vice President of the local hospital where most of the women were receiving care and treatment. As a long time meditation teacher I have been invited to lead a meditation with this group. I feel totally inadequate and humbled in the face of both their suffering and their courage. I tell them so and then we proceed to do a check in, going around the circle for those that want to say something to the group about why they are there and how they are doing. It is even more humbling, almost overwhelming for me as I am the only seemingly "healthy" one in the room.

"Each of the women presented her circumstances and challenges in a matter of fact and mostly neutral tone. One young lady tells us that she's going blind. Another, older woman shares that her cancer is at stage four and she doesn't have long to live. Others describe elements of their battle, while still others talk about their families and loved ones. All speak with courage and wisdom that I cannot fathom. I do my best to hold back tears of admiration and compassion and lead the group in a meditation. They take to it quickly and suddenly the room is full of an ineffable Light I have only felt on very rare occasions.

"These women have all faced death imminently or it is knocking and threatening at the door. For the most part, each of them is rising above it to a higher plane of existence and reality. The flow of conversation when we debrief the meditation is easy, relaxed, and enlightening. Their casual wisdom and Light in the face of disease and death was seared into my being that day. Years later, when I faced my own battle with an advanced and aggressive cancer, I used the memory and taste of their wisdom to guide me to my own Higher place. I am so grateful for the better angels of their Being, which have become a guiding Light for me for the rest of my life.

"This event profoundly affected my thinking about and approach to meditation and sharing from this space as I realized the power of community and connection. These women did not know one another, and yet they did. A few moments together in safe, sacred space, allowed them to share and learn in very new ways. With the vulnerability of their truth self evident and their egos faded into the background, they were able to connect across age, culture and circumstance. I began to see meditation as an act of community rather than isolation."

Imaginal Calisthenics

This third and final summation from Brooks Cole speaks to the impact of doing Wacuri Journeys on a regular basis:

"To me, some of the most valuable results of Wacuri journeys are the ways they stretch and tone my imagination. I'm pretty sure that regular giving, receiving and sharing of these brief but potent journeys can demonstrably strengthen the powers of one's imagination. I have certainly found this to be so after having participated in the giving and receiving of over 200 journeys to date.

"As a teenager growing up in Colorado, seeking escape, I was fascinated by intelligence, dreams, memory, and reverie. I sensed that these were all somehow connected by the acuity of the mind's eye. I learned early on how different types of stimuli could catalyze flights of imagination. Pink Floyd (or similarly evocative music of the time), a beanbag chair and headphones became my vehicle for endless cosmic exploration with my young imagination. I also read voraciously and found certain books to be especially visually transporting. Steadily, I began to realize that the more vivid and immersive the pictures in my mind became, the happier and more creative I became, and the better I did in school. I began to notice the correlation between the vividness of my mental pictures and my ability to remember concepts or to summon the right words or ideas when speaking or writing. Early on in high school, I began to experiment with mnemonic techniques. When I had to memorize many groups of facts in order to ace a particular test, I learned to create encoded mental images to recall at test time—people or things in strange situations, balancing stacks of objects or situations, each representing an idea (the more preposterous, the easier to remember). It worked like a charm. And it exercised my imagination. Increasingly, I began to understand the mind space as an addressable expanse where storage and retrieval could be enhanced with the imagination.

"Fast forward to today, I have joined the other Wacuri founders in experiencing or leading several journeys a week for over two years, and can report unequivocally that repeated journeys enhance and strengthen the imagination. Each journey takes the participant, and even the Journey Guide giving the journey, on a flight of imagination. The giver urges the participants to see, hear, feel and touch all manner of details and sensations that exist only in their imaginations. Particularly striking, looking back over all these journeys, is the vastness of dimensions of this imaginal universe. We have journeyed across the universe of time, space, and scale, matter and energy and life. We've explored the macrocosm—from the birth of stars, galaxies and distant worlds to flights over every kind of landscape; the microcosm—from the consciousness of cells to DNA and atoms and photons; the infocosm—from historical figures and places to ideas of all kinds; to emotions from fear to love and joy, to time travel and so much more. This has felt to me like a giant imaginal gymnasium for exercising and toning the ability to drop into a state of vivid imagination whenever needed.

"Each time I enjoy a Wacuri journey, I experience a greater capacity to use my mind's eye and my heart's grasp. And each time I share my experience with others, or listen to their sharing, I feel a deeper connection to others with my essential humanness. This is what I call imaginal calisthenics, an exercise to increase your connectedness with others and give your imagination a remarkable workout."

Sample Sharings

To give you a sense of how people share their experience after a journey, we have included here a couple of transcripts of actual debriefs.

This first debrief features shares from Henry and Brooks after they went on the Journey to the Consciousness of Cells. Note how quickly the debriefs can be done.

Henry: I started with some cells inside of my nose. Initially, they felt like bright sparkles, then I felt them spreading as my whole body started coming alive in the light. And then I felt that light extend to people, other people that I know, and then it extended out to all the trees and animals and then to everything in the universe. I felt all coming to life. And all of that grew from the cells in the end of my nose.

Brooks: I revisited the scenes in the Toy Story movies where these little fluff-ball guys have a kind of hive mind. I remember how these little alien fluffy creatures are scrambling around in the machine and praying to "the claw." I saw fields and fields of cells on this rolling landscape that were kind of like these alien creatures because they were all singing, they were singing in waves and lighting up. The propagation of the light moved through them as if in waves, in concentric waves, out across the landscape following the curvatures of the tissues and skins and organs of which they are a part. And I heard the most marvelous harmonic singing, it was almost like the music of the spheres, coming out of all these little high-pitched voices of all these happy cells. And now, I feel happy, as if my soul is singing.

This second debrief features shares from Adam and Henry after they went on the Journey to the Heart Center. Note how the Journey Guide (Dan Spinner) encourages the participants to share the feeling elicited by the journey.

Adam: I noticed that my heart center had a certain density in the middle that went further in. It got more and more dense until there was no real delineation as it seemed to move out past my shoulders, out in front of me, and beside me. It was kind of whitish in color on the outside and yellowish where it became more dense. From the center to the periphery this field emanating from my heart kept the same beat as my physical heart. This gave me a feeling of warmth and a certain tangible sense of being connected to other people, not all things necessarily, but definitely other people.

Dan: What would you say your emotional state was or is?

Adam: Very calm. When you said think of someone you love I noticed that swirls of red and blue, like sort of Pollock-swirls, went inside of my heart like a combination of joy and sadness, although I wasn't actually thinking of anyone in particular.

Dan: Henry?

Henry: When I went there, I thought, it kind of started out as white, and it quickly turned green, kind of green and glowing, like kind of sphere but, at the same time, kind of a star. It had points coming out at 90 degrees all the way around, coming out on the top and bottom, just like a star. It kept changing colors to yellow and blue and becoming larger, and it was pulsing similar to my heart. Then it got larger and larger, until it was larger than my body, larger even than the planet. I felt like my heart center was out beyond the universe; it just seemed like it was penetrating everything.

When you asked us to think of someone, I thought about Maria, her energy and her heart, and how I love her, I just, I felt it. I felt calm, I still feel calm. I feel like I'm floating. In joy...it's kind of a joy feeling of just being connected. Thinking about bringing that kind of connectedness into my day, I thought YES, I want to feel that."

Dan: I should have known, Henry, when I found myself saying make it as large as you want, you would make it as large as the universe. And you know, when we journey to these centers, the heart as well as the others, it's an act of integration, taking the energetic aspects of our beings, exploring them and integrating with our psyches and our physical bodies, and so the act of taking into the workplace or with a loved one, either in or near our reality or imagination changes things. For example, just try to imagine if you can being in your heart center and being mad at someone. Or annoyed. It won't happen. Or perhaps imagine being annoyed or mad at someone, but opening up your heart center for the annoyance or anger. When that other person, colleague, friend, partner, learns about the heart center, then good for them, then think about, just as you implied Henry, think about the power of doing that with your family or your kids. Imagine teaching your kids about the heart center. There are many, many applications. It's just fun to explore.

Dan: Other comments or questions for one another?

LONG PAUSE

Dan: Think about your own relationship. And the homework is to try it. Just play with it. Maybe when you are in a pretty good place, but when you are not in a good place, you might want to try it too. How are you each feeling now?

Henry: I'm feeling you know, just sedate.

Adam: Pleasant and a little bit excited to try this out both with my daughter and with a couple of friends of ours.

Henry: Maybe I'll try it with one or both of my boys.

A Multiverse of Journeys

Many traditional mindfulness practices recommend performing the same exercise every day. In contrast, the Wacuri Method encourages the spontaneous creation of new subjects each time, within the basic structure of the method. Journey participants are free to take an entirely different journey each time. Or, they can choose to repeat a journey they like, go deeper into it and/or invite a friend to join them on the journey.

This lack of a disciplined, single minded point of focus may seem to be a weakness to those who favor traditional mindfulness practices. However, we have found it to be a strength. Unlike a mindfulness practice that seeks to still the thoughts completely, the Wacuri Method involves a rich exercise of the mind through imagination and guided journeys. Like traditional mindfulness, the journeyers experience is non-verbal during the journey itself. It is up to the Journey Guide to construct a verbal experience and then, after the journey, to invite participants to speak during the sharing.

There are no limits to the subjects of the meditations. We often use animals, insects such as a bumblebee, or even a Spider web. These elements of nature tend to invoke awe. Other journeys focus on supposedly inanimate objects that often reveal themselves as totally alive. One of our authors, Rob Read, is a computer scientist. He sometimes leads journeys to abstract, non-physical subjects such as the Realm of Mathematics. Some of the most powerful journeys are psychological, such as Journey to the Inner Child or Journey to the Transformation of Fear.

By celebrating the diversity of such subjects, it is necessarily the case that not every journey will resonate with every journeyer. In general, each journeyer gets varying amounts of insight and experience in different dimensions of the psyche from each journey. Not every experience will be a peak experience. Sometimes in the debrief, one person will share that the journey was mildly interesting only to discover that the same journey was riveting for another journeyer, perhaps due to their past experience or a difference in their personality. One person's understanding and affinity for Dark Matter or the Inner Child may be completely different than that of another person. It's important to realize that journeys are not lectures meant to convey scientifically accurate information but rather artistic explorations. It is not important that a journey cover or not cover the particulars of any given topic, rather that the journey elicit an emotional response in the both the Journey Guide and those being led on the journey. The value of any given journey lies solely in its effect, the impact it has on those who experience it. In future, we plan to invite the Wacuri community to recommend new journey topics so the library of journeys will be endless, extensive, and ever growing.

CHAPTER ELEVEN

HALLMARKS OF AWAKENING

A human being is a part of the whole, called by us "Universe," a part limited in time and space. He experiences himself, his thoughts and feelings as something separate from the rest—a kind of optical delusion of his consciousness. The striving to free oneself from this delusion is the one issue of true religion. Not to nourish it but to try to overcome it is the way to reach the attainable measure of peace of mind.

~Albert Einstein

We've all heard of sudden spiritual awakenings. Consider the unhappy housewife with an alcohol problem who wakes up in a treatment center staring at an insect and has a massive epiphany. The nature of mind suddenly becomes clear to her. She realizes a profound truth beyond and behind what we think of as "real" and her life is never the same. She goes on to develop The Work of Byron Katie and develop an international following.

A gay man, celebrated author, and right-hand to a renowned guru, is bereft when his boyfriend leaves him. In the depth of his grief, he awakens to the Ultimate Truth. He eventually leaves his guru and becomes a world teacher in his own right. We are speaking, of course, of beloved Andrew Harvey.

Then there is the German fellow who had been depressed for years, was dangerously close to becoming homeless, and started contemplating suicide. Then, one afternoon, something remarkable happens. He suddenly had a profound realization. He gets enlightenment in a flash of insight and his life is forever changed. The world knows this man as the popular spiritual teacher, Eckhart Tolle.

In Tolle's own words:

"I was unhappy, depressed and anxious. I was not trying to become enlightened or anything like that. I was looking for some kind of answer to the dilemma of life, but I had been looking to the intellect for the answer… I reached a point where the phrase came into my head… 'I can't live with myself any longer.' That part of my self — that entity became so heavy and painful."

"Suddenly I stepped back from myself, and it seemed to be two of me — The 'I,' and this 'self' that I cannot live with. Am I one or am I two? And that triggered me like a koan. It happened to me spontaneously. I looked at that sentence — 'I can't live with myself.' I had no intellectual answer. Who am I? Who is this self that I cannot live with? The answer came on a deeper level. I realized who I was… What 'I' as consciousness had identified with was a very heavy mental and emotional form consisting of thought and accompanied by an energy field. At that moment the identification with that mind structure was withdrawn. It collapsed, and what remained was a spacious, peaceful consciousness… I had been anxious and depressed for years and suddenly I was deeply at peace."

Gaining An Internal Compass

Stories such as Katie's, Harvey's, and Tolle's can lead us to believe that awakening occurs in a moment of sudden, all-pervasive realization, or what our friend Neal Rogan calls "thunderstanding." More often than not, however, awakening happens slowly over time. It begins when an individual is ready for a growth spurt. In the early stage, awakening is usually vague. Not always, mind you. Sometimes waking up can be very specific. A good example of this is the classic conversion experience that happened to the founders of Alcoholics Anonymous. But a life-changing psycho-spiritual conversion typically happens bit-by-bit as a person revises their view of themselves and the world, and develops a new relationship with time.

This bit-by-bit progression has some predictability. There is a natural sequence to the process that spiritual teachers around the world will map out for you. As with all explorations into new terrain, having a map of the territory can be useful. But having a compass is even better. Maps are static. Their usefulness is limited in a world of constant change. The Wacuri Method can turn your inbuilt, curious nature into a compass that you can rely on for direction in any circumstance, everyday and extraordinary alike.

Tapping Into A Greater Force

Awakening is an inner journey that begins with looking inside. That's where the real journey happens. On the inside. The Wacuri Method is designed to take you into your innermost terrain where you may very well stumble into a vastness far beyond what you can currently imagine.

Our aim is to shift the way in which you look, the place from which you look and, ultimately, the manner of seeing that informs all of your senses. Every one of the hundreds of Wacuri journeys, is, in this sense, the same journey — the journey within.

Go inside yourself on a regular basis, and you will make a remarkable discovery. From within your very consciousness, you can access the vastness of the entire cosmos. Once you have gained access, you can tap into a greater force. You'll start to see a miraculous new world rise up before you.

Our young culture is slowly beginning to recognize the value of the inner search recommended by the ancients and to celebrate the passion that arises from that search. And while our culture at large has yet to reward the search in any substantial way, the riches one gains are undeniable. You gain genuine spiritual and energetic passion, a sense of aliveness that is the exclusive purview of those engaged in this penultimate endeavor. Whereas you may have spent years consumed with worldly concerns like making money, over-consuming, gaining status, or caught up in addiction, you begin rising up out of those pursuits. The rising up generally begins with some kind of inquiry.

Inquiry and curiosity are the hallmarks of awakening. These are delicate moments. When someone has an "Oh my God" moment of realization, it's significant. Those moments deserve our loving attention. Lots of it.

The Wacuri Method is designed to support your awakening with a technique that allows you to discover what you're truly passionate about. The call to Wake Up Curious meets the need for a reward system that supports your awakening. There are cultures that have rewards systems in place for that. Mainstream culture tends to stifle, even punish, genuine inquiry. It is certainly set up to distract us from the search at every turn. Your peers may actually poo-poo it. "Why not just be like everyone else? Keep making money. Get that new Lexus. Let's go out and pound down a few beers. Get back on the dating horse. Forget about her, life goes on."

But something deep inside you knows better. Moments of passion, inquiry, and curiosity, rise up from that place deep inside.

Self Knowledge and Surrender

We've all heard the Serenity Prayer: "God, grant me the serenity to accept the things I cannot change, the courage to change the things I can, and the wisdom to know the difference." Authored by American theologian Reinhold Niebuhr (1892-1971), the prayer was first recited in a sermon Niebuhr delivered at the Evangelical Church in Heath, Massachusetts. Alcoholics Anonymous adopted the prayer in 1941 and it was later canonized by Kurt Vonnegut in *Slaughterhouse Five*. Few are the prayers that pack so much wisdom into a single sentence.

Anyone who has developed the ability to "accept the things I cannot change" has acquired some degree of self-knowledge. Aiming at perfection and imagining that one day we will "arrive" are habits of mind that arise from the false self. Those who cannot surrender tend to hold onto a vision of themselves that just plain ain't so. As we begin to awaken, these mental constructs lose their grip. Accepting "what's so" rather than remaining invested in self-delusions, and false assumptions requires faith and the ability to trust the unknown. We begin to accept ourselves, recognize our human failings, and accept that other people are also flawed. The uninitiated tend to assume that acceptance makes people lazy and complacent. This is a mistaken impression.

Acceptance liberates a tremendous amount of energy, energy that can bring about an unprecedented psycho-spiritual transformation.

We are, at times, our own worst enemy. Taking stock, deciding what we can change about ourselves, and dedicating ourselves to make those changes takes courage and tenacity. Surrender and acceptance, once again, are key. When we accept that hardships lead to growth and learn to surrender our attachment to a preferred outcome, we find peace of mind, even in the midst of turmoil.

The word "surrender" has a negative connotation. In certain contexts it means to succumb, give up, or capitulate. People tend to associate the word with failure or victimhood. In this context, however, to elegantly surrender is an act of self-empowerment. We let go of digging in our heels and let the Powers That Be show us a friendly universe. We exchange our "someday maybe" approach to life for inner peace and self-knowledge in the now.

Self-responsibility: Your Greatest Asset

One of the surprising aspects of awakening is the freedom that comes with taking full responsibility for our state of mind and body. This includes being responsible for the impact we have on others. Taking responsibility for our situation, even situations where we're in tremendous pain, requires us to re-contextualize our reality. Consider, for example, a person who finds him or herself in jail. They are stuck in a cell, perhaps even in a foreign country, feeling desperate and alone. How in the heck does a person re-contextualize that?!? Wouldn't such a circumstance weigh in at the very bottom on the scale of well-being? It seems reasonable to assume so — until and unless we shift our attention from the circumstance itself to the way we relate to the circumstance. The best way to do that is to ask the question: "What are my priorities now? What is my attitude given that I'm in jail?" By asking these questions, we are taking responsibility for how we show up in the situation. That involves creating a very specific personal context for our circumstances. Nelson Mandela is a powerful example of how this can be accomplished.

The more awake we are, the more aware we become that we're living inside of assumed contexts. A context is an invisible story that has no chance of becoming visible until we acknowledge what we've been telling ourselves. For the most part, the contexts we live in are not generated by the individual. They are pre-existing paradigms we're born into and/or are marinated in every day. They include memes, assumptions and storylines about scarcity, good and bad, right or wrong that shape our thoughts and determine how we view reality. If we've bought into the right/wrong paradigm, it is easy to look at another and say, "There's something wrong." In doing so, we say, "It's not my responsibility." But what if simply being part of this world means it is my responsibility? Say you're in Iran riding in a taxi. The driver is speeding but you say nothing and he causes an accident. Are you responsible? It depends on the paradigm. In Iran, you would be held responsible simply because you hired the driver.

Taking responsibility means accepting the proposition that we all create our own reality, for better or worse. If this is true, we can ask ourselves, in each moment of surrender to the current reality, "What am I trying to teach myself?"

Imagine that you are completely the author of every aspect of your reality. That is true self responsibility. Paradoxically, when we surrender to this and accept all that is implied, a higher flow emerges. We avail ourselves of a vast source of power that is inaccessible prior to our surrender. In this way, self-surrender and self-responsibility merge and morph into an exquisite, co-creative relationship with the Universe itself.

Connected Co-Creative Intelligence

As a deeper understanding of the transmissive patterns and possibilities of the Wacuri Method emerges, a new manner of transmission arises with a corresponding heightened receptivity in certain listeners. This development gives the impression of a slipstream that generates a stronger, clearer experience for the listener. It's as though the Journey Guide can swing open the door to multidimensional realities and invite those taking the journey to cross the threshold and enter the subtle realms. Ultimately, the whole purpose of opening the door is for the individual to grow their own consciousness so they can open the door of their own accord. How different would your life be if you developed this skill and had the ability to access connected, co-creative intelligence whenever you choose to do so?

Experienced Journey Guides can architect a finer and higher set of energies in the transmissive process. As usual, this involves some trial and error. Advanced practitioners can feel and, in an oddly non-visual way, see into the architecture of resonant field biofeedback loops. Dan Spinner experiences them as arcs made up of Light that arise out of the material world and curve back into the Infinite in much the same way as a rainbow appears in atmosphere and curves back to Earth. These arcs vary in their dimensionality and characteristics (presumably due to differing frequencies and tones), and they intersect and entwine with other arcs in an organic, eternal, harmonious dance of motion and music. Glimpsed briefly or from afar, the dance initially appears chaotic, but when felt into and observed closely, they reveal a choreography so elegant and extraordinary as to actually generate a resonant harmonic field that can be felt.

Perhaps the entrée point into the slipstream is when the Journey Guide can hold the increasing energy levels of these intersecting arcs of Light as if they were tuning forks or sacred crystal bowls. Is it so outlandish to consider that the universe is made up of music? That celestial music is real? And is there is an orchestral harmony to all of this at some level? Could a human being learn to conduct and co-create the ever-shifting tones? Certainly, the Journey Guides would need to be extremely resilient and adaptable, able to find the center at every moment, track the subtle shifts, and the through-line of each emerging tone and tune.

Would the guide him or herself then become an instrument of the divine? An orchestra leader or conductor who is both following and being guided by the unseen? Would s/he then be both conductor and listener, receiver and transmitter?

What if these orchestrations exist at higher and deeper levels to infinity? Perhaps the music gets more and more exquisite with each next level in the dance.

We know from experience that sensing sacred geometric and graphically precise patterns allows for the realization and experience of higher vibrations and finer and finer "musical" tunes. At the same time, science has shown convincingly that when you regard something it regards you, which is to say the bio-feedback loop between Journey Guide and participant(s) can be quite powerful. And the resonant strength of the shared biofield opens up tremendous possibilities by tapping into our Inner Wisdom. Curiouser and curiouser, yes?

Perhaps sitting in the midst of all those flows, known and unknown, while holding that shared space is the key that opens the door to a multidimensional existence beyond our wildest imaginings. Perhaps in addition to conducting thought experiments, we can begin to conduct flow experiments. As more individuals grow their awareness of this higher form of intelligence, we foresee a time when their subtle perceptual capacity becomes keen and highly refined. This is a developmental process that occurs over time, of course. As people become accustomed to receiving ever-deeper transmissions, the transmissions become tangible, akin to "white noise" humming audibly in the background. Skilled Journey Guides may even discover that they can lend sound or texture to journeys.

These are the potentials we see on the horizon for advanced practitioners who take on the Wake Up Curious approach to social meditation.

Stardust and Light

Suppose that we have it all backwards? We tend to presuppose that the material world dominates and the ephemeral is an afterthought to be explored when everything is quiet.

Suppose it is not that way at all. Suppose we are manifestations of the subtle energies we sometimes intuit around us. That we live under a grand illusion that material reality, and therefore our very own bodies, are the key element of the Universe. Said that way it sounds a little pretentious, doesn't it? Perhaps the reality is much different. Perhaps our version of reality is untrue, like "the earth is flat" conceit or the notion that all circles around us. Perhaps the biofield energies "around" our bodies are actually the energies that produce and hold the field for the creation of our bodies.

Whether we know it or not, there seems to be a biofield-based "shimmer" all around us. And this shimmer also seems to be all around everything: each tree, each rock, each cell, each atom. In this scenario, everything changes. If we truly understand this, we begin to suspect that our very existence is created by the shimmer, not the other way around.

What is this shimmer? This biofield? Where does it come from? How would we live if the notion that the shimmer "creates" us was accepted as true? How would that change us? The change could be quite profound when we come to understand that it is the same substance for all and that we share these invisible energy fields.

What if we could look in the mirror and know for certain that stardust and Light binds us all in an intricate dance of Harmony?

Shimmer Everywhere

On the edge of our vision just out of reach
Is a glimmer
A twitch, a sense of something else
A faint glow that is often barely noticed
But always there when we look…
If we look.
Rushing through our daily efforts we often don't

Breathlessly, we dash to whatever it is that captures
our small minds
Noticing hardly anything never mind the subtle
Still it's there
Surrounding us wherever we are and however we
are
Like an unknown companion
A second skin a few feet away from the first one
Moving, dynamic, ephemeral, just out of grasp....
But still there.
A Shimmer, filaments of silver and gold so fine as to
almost be invisible
A Shimmer that can comfort and hold us
A Shimmer that can inform and illuminate
A Shimmer that connects to everything
Others, Trees, Rocks, Oceans and beyond.
They have their own Shimmer too
And perhaps our Shimmers meet up
In sacred harmony and vibratory exchange
A sort of Community of Shimmering.
A total connection of all that thinks it is separate.
The Shimmer may be the level of reality through
which
The Divine Light appears
Sustaining us and our capacities to Love and spread
Light
And even the very manner in which form itself
manifests.
~ Dan Spinner

When we Wake Up Curious together and share our experience in deep resonance and presence with one another, the shimmer is shared — a group biofield — and thus somehow stronger, more felt and known by all. We come into a deeper connection with self, others and the Universe. This is our response and answer to existential loneliness. This is the cyber-sangha of the Wake Up Curious community, waking up curious together.

Appendix A

Curious.live Platform Research and Development

Wacuri is conducting research and development on tools and technologies to practice deeper connections. We are open to collaboration with user researchers and designers and front-end and back-end developers. See https://github.com/Wacuri/wacurimvp to look under the hood, follow our progress and/or join our community of collaborators.

Wacuri is using agile practices, which prioritize people over process. For this, we are working with personal growth practitioners who are early adopters of technology. If you would like to join us in developing easy to use emerging technologies, please email us at info@wacuri.com with your contact information and a paragraph describing how you would like to participate.

Early Focus Areas:

The curious.live journey board: One of the advantages of taking a journey with another person is similar to teaming up with a workout buddy. You get the social benefit of camaraderie and motivation, the psychological benefit of being heard and seen, and the neurological benefit of practicing verbalizing introspective concepts. The curious.live platform eliminates the need to go out and find that person; the platform "journey board" does it for you. Similarly, the platform solves the difficult problem of scheduling a convenient time for two or more busy people. Even a mere fifteen minutes can be difficult to find, but the platform lets you find partners to connect with on the fly, whenever you have a window of free time and feel inspired to meditate and share the experience with someone else.

The curious.live research platform uses videoconferencing, which allows participants to experience live journeys together. The journey board features recorded audio journeys to give as many people as possible the Wacuri experience. Although a real-time experience with a Journey Guide is sometimes preferable, the recorded journeys also carry the transmission and the platform creates a structured place and time to share after the journey to practice verbalizing emotional insights with other people. Even though the guide is not live, the participants have a live experience of each other. Whether that is by mobile phone, computer-based audio, or computer-based video, participants get to practice sharing and listening and experience a sense of "togetherness". Video conferencing such as that provided by Skype, Zoom, and Google Hangouts are quite useful in this regard. Furthermore, as a best practice, participants should leave their cameras and audio on, even if they are not speaking or moving during the journey. The sharing afterward benefits from audio and visual contact as it allows participants to listen deeply to one another. You want to listen as deeply as possible to each participant in an effort to connect at a level more authentic and beyond the normal level of human interaction.

In time, the platform may be extended to track key biometrics such as pulse, HRV, and breathing rate, as well as directly measure brain waves and other patterns in response to both the journeys and the sharing. We are actively looking for partners to develop and test these extensions.

In keeping with the spirit of our mission to create greater connection and abundance, our platform is free-libre open source, which means anyone may examine our code and reuse it, even for commercial purposes, so long as their improvements are also made freely available to all. Our source code is licensed under the GNU Affero General Public License (https://www.gnu.org/licenses/agpl-3.0.en.html), and is freely downloadable (https://github.com/Wacuri/wacurimvp). The art work and trademarks may not be reused without our permission.

Appendix B

The Journey Guide School

The Wacuri Method depends on the Journey Guide, the person who uses spoken word to create the journey. The Journey is not written out or even outlined beforehand, rather, it is spontaneously transmitted, which means the guide shares their own feelings and energy with the listener. A journey is an improv performance, not a composition or a script. The Guide allows the topic of any given meditation to elicit the feelings, thoughts, and impressions that make up the journey. The Journey Guide School features a specific curriculum devoted to explaining this process and sharing the best practices and techniques we have discovered to help those who wish to guide Wacuri journeys to do so successfully.

The goal of a Journey Guide is to awaken curiosity and, if possible, a sense of awe in the journeyer. This could be accomplished by writing, drawing, or with a photograph, however, the Wacuri Method is a unique technique. Rather than evocative practices like creative writing, slam poetry, or oral storytelling, all of which are powerful arts, the Wacuri Method sees the Journey as flowing from the source of the topic through the Guide to the journeyer. In other words, a Wacuri Journey is more than spoken words, it is a process of transmission.

Rather than construct an intellectual endeavor like those present in an academic setting, the goal is to authentically convey — with minimum artifice — the thoughts, feelings, and awe of Source directly. The process is similar to a jazz improvisation, altogether different than playing a written piece of music.

To do this, the Guide learns how to center him or herself and achieve a flow state. They are taught to invoke something larger than themselves, then open to the topic of the meditation. At that point the topic becomes the active subject of the meditation. It is also the source of conveyed or transmitted images, thoughts, impressions, sensations and feelings.

Wacuri Journeys are never scripted or rehearsed. They are completely spontaneous or "live" every time there are produced. To enable this, prior to commencing a Wacuri Journey, guides learn to prepare themselves by becoming as centered and present as possible. This allows the Guide to enter into a higher flow where they can readily connect with the Journey topic. Sometimes the guide chooses the topic, the topic may also be spontaneous, or they may take requests from the journeyers, asking if they have someplace they'd like to go.

The key is to allow spontaneity to flow through the Journey structure, allowing for personalized variations and experimentation as the guide is inclined. Although it may seem counterintuitive at first, the structure actually holds the journey together, making it cohesive. By allowing for variation within that structure, the content can be organic. This encourages authenticity in the moment and a deeper transmission of the content or subject. When the Journey Guide is in a state of high flow s/he can take the feeling of the subject matter into their imagination and effectively channel the content and words they find flowing out of them. This requires an ability to stay in each moment as it unfolds without leaping ahead mentally in anticipation of what to say next. This is a crucial part of the Wacuri Method.

Let's look at an example. Say the source of the journey is a tree. The guide begins by feeling a tree intensely. A practice that can help achieve this intensity is to recall the most powerful memory you have of a tree—perhaps a favorite tree you climbed as a child. The key is to connect deeply with the feeling of the tree. If the object is one that you have no direct experience with, say a black hole, you still connect to the imagined power, energy, majesty and danger of a black hole. It is better to do this without verbally listing various aspects of the tree or black hole in your mind. You are not composing a lecture, you are transmitting impressions from the source. This may be emotionally challenging as well as mentally difficult. For example, if the source is the Transformation of Fear or Recovery from Addiction, the guide must feel the fear or compulsion and be prepared to convey that before transmitting relief from the fear or freedom from compulsion.

After the Journey Guide has mentally connected with the source, he or she must connect with the journeyers. Even if making a recording, guides imagine the journeyers while becoming a conduit for transmitting from the source to the journeyer.

Once the guide feels both the source and journeyer, they are ready to begin.

The Journey Guide School outlines the basic structure of the journey, which should be considered an important guideline. Other tips to keep in mind include:

Invite your journeyers to vividly connect to the source. It may help to use sensory and emotional language.

Give the journeyers permission to construct their own version of the source by saying "You choose…" or "You pick…." Precision quickens writing, but is not needed in transmission. You may find yourself giving precise details, while leaving some aspects of the source unspoken or unspecified.

Try to transmit partially verbally and partially emotionally. It is not necessary to reduce all information to words. Guides generally find the source gives them an avalanche of words that far exceed what can be transmitted fully. Be judicious about what you say.

Silences are golden and necessary. Pauses are needed for the journeyers to connect to the source in their own imagination. Pauses also give the guide a chance to sense the strongest impression to transmit from the source.

Fill silences with emotion, not sound. When you pause, you should still feel your connection to the source as compellingly as possible and imagine this same connection to your journeyers.

Just as you should love someone not just when you say "I love you!" but before and after this exclamation, you should try to connect to your source and journeyers ahead of time and follow through with some mental energy after the journey. This does not have to be specific. For example, you may not know the topic ahead of time, but you can still imagine a successful connection between the source and journeyers.

Finally, you may want to watch for delightful surprises as a marker for your success. If in a journey to a flower you find yourself surprised by something you say that was unplanned— perhaps the life of a spider residing in the flower—this is a good sign that you have achieved the desired spontaneity of flow.

Deeper connections with Self,
Others and the Universe

Curious.live or Wacuri (which means Wake Up Curious) enables people to make deep connections quickly and easily through five-minute guided mindfulness journeys followed by sharing their experiences and discoveries. Participants report greater energy and alignment with others, team cohesion, and personal breakthroughs in mood, creativity and greater well-being after both the meditations and the sharing. Curious.live journeys have been listened to almost 60,000 times by an audience of over 25,000 people on Insight Timer, a meditation service used by approximately 7 million people!

https://curious.live

Thank You !

Thank You For Reading My Book!

I really appreciate all of your feedback, and I love hearing what you have to say.

I need your input to make the next version of this book and my future books even better.

Please leave me a helpful review on Amazon letting me know what you thought of the book.

Thank you so much!
Wacuri Publishing